ANGEL BUMPS

Hello from Heaven

———◆———

COMPILED BY

ANNE BARDSLEY

Mill Park Publishing
Eagle, Idaho

Mill Park Publishing
www.MillParkPublishing.com

Mill Park Publishing
www.MillParkPublishing.com

ISBN: 978-0-9975871-1-1
Printed in USA
Mill Park Publishing
Eagle, ID 83616
www.MillParkPublishing.com

I dedicate this book to my Mom,
my angel and my best friend
who continues to love me from Heaven.

Contents

Contents, continued.

Acknowledgements

Angel Bumps has been published in my mind, years ago. When I'd meet someone in a cloud of grief, I'd tell them the story of my mom sending me a sign of a small white butterfly. Actually, her sign was a blizzard of butterflies that surrounded my car when I asked her for a sign. I know that my mom's spirit is alive and well. A white butterfly has arrived at special occasions throughout the years. When I tell people that story, it seems to bring comfort. Some will say they have goose bumps. Others dry their eyes and hug me; some will say, "You should write a book!" I thank them for their inspiration.

I owe thanks to each person who submitted a story. Some of their stories are very personal and touching. A few were very hard for them to write. I honor them for sharing their stories.

My husband, Scott, is my favorite person on earth. I couldn't ask for a sweeter man. When I am incensed with my computer, forget passwords, and delete files, he calmly rescues me. I think he does magic, honestly. He pushed me to complete this book to help people with their grief. I liken it to having a baby. He's my birth coach and it's time for delivery. Where's my epidural?

I'd like to thank my family and friends, who always checked in and asked how this book was coming along. They're also my marketing team, spreading news before it's even published. I love each and every one of them.

I'd especially like to thank Karen Fox Tarlton of Karen's Fine Arts for her permission to use her painting for the cover of this book. She is so talented and her painting touches my heart.

I'd like to thank Sarah del Rio for her editing skills. She is very gifted. Bless her heart.

Elaine Ambrose has been invaluable with her editing and publishing. When I grow up I am going to be just like her. I admire her tenacity, humor, and her talent. I genuinely love her.

I want to thank God, my angels and all of those who have sent signs of love from Heaven. You touch my heart, amaze me with your love, make me smile... and even shed a few tears.

I am one, very blessed, lady.

My friends, I wish you many angel bumps!

Introduction

I am a believer. I believe in the afterlife. I believe loved ones who have passed send us signs to connect with us from the other side. There is something life-changing that happens when you realize that you've received a sign from someone who has passed. Your world opens to the possibility that they are still with you, even though it's just in spirit.

The feeling that accompanies an angel bump is usually soothing and loving. Some may make you cry, smile, or even laugh out loud. Usually the angel bump is a sentimental moment; especially when you realize they are still so close. When I experienced my first, I was over the moon excited. Just because I can't see them physically, doesn't mean they aren't with me spiritually.

Signs are unique, just like people. Some of the most common signs are:
>   *Birds (especially cardinals)*
>   *butterflies*
>   *a song on the radio dream*

> *a vision*
> *missing items*
> *electrical disturbances*
> *a license plate that might match a significant date*
> *sudden gusts of wind when there is no wind in the air*
> *a fragrance*
> *an article of clothing like the person wore.*

Children often have visions or feelings about someone who has passed away. The reasoning is that their minds are still close to the spirit world and haven't been tainted. If a child tells you about a sign they received, just listen. Their signs are usually pure and simple, but very detailed.

If, by some chance, you don't recognize a sign, I believe it will come again. Sometimes we just aren't open to the possibility of little connections that happen around us. Other times, we are just so busy. You need to slow down and pay attention so they can connect with you. It will bring you joy.

Stories in this book will charm you. We are kindred spirits who believe in love from beyond. If this book can help open your mindset, just a smidge, I think you may start to notice signs you previously dismissed. It's not a scary thing, by any means.

Once you realize that you've been bumped by an angel, a wonderful thing happens. It's like a very bright light went on in a dark room. I believe that reaction makes our loved ones equally happy. They want us to know they are still with us.

I hope you enjoy this book. Each story has been shared with love.

I wish you many angel bumps in your future.

Blessings!

A Little White Butterfly
Anne Bardsley

A week after my mom passed, I was driving to my gift store, Anne's House of Angels, when I asked her for a sign that she had made it to Heaven. I felt a hand rest on my cheek, and I smiled and said: "What the heck was that, Mom?"

Then I wondered if it had really happened. I asked, "Mom, can you send me a real sign? As I turned the corner, my car was instantly engulfed in little white butterflies. It was a butterfly blizzard! I cried, and I laughed. I could almost hear her giggling and saying, "Anne, did you get that sign you asked for? Was that one real enough for you?"

Ever since that day, when I think of my mom, a little white butterfly appears. At my angel store, it became a tradition that if anyone spotted a white butterfly in the rose bushes out front, they would run in and tell me, "Anne, your mom's out front again!" I loved that sisterhood, and the total belief in her sign.

My mom's sign as a little white butterfly isn't surprising. She wasn't a flashy woman; she wouldn't need to be a fancy, multi-colored butterfly. She wouldn't want big, ostentatious wings. Small, classic, delicate wings were just her style. She lived her life with simple pleasures, and now she continues to bless my life in the same fashion.

⌒∽∽⌒

When my son finished high school, I was distraught that my mom couldn't be with us to attend the graduation ceremony. It was the first big family celebration since she passed. I sat down in the rocking chair on my front porch, in tears.

Just then a little butterfly landed in my hanging basket. It bounced to the next one and finally, onto my chair. I sniffled and said, "Hi, Mom. I'm really missing you today."

When it was time to go, my family walked to the car, and the white butterfly came along, dancing around each one of us. My daughters said in unison, "Nan's here!" And she *was* there, circling the car. She flitted in front of the windshield to be sure we all noticed her.

My husband asked, "Did you really think she'd miss her grandson's graduation?"

Of course I didn't.

⌒∽∽⌒

She continued her visits. At the rehearsal for my son's garden wedding, my husband and I sat in the front row. Times like that always made me miss both of my parents. I was taking a sentimental journey in my mind when a small white butterfly arrived. She danced between the future bride and groom as they practiced their vows. She lingered, watching from a branch. I like to think she was sprinkling them with blessings for their life together.

She would never miss her grandson's wedding.

⁓⁓⁓

These small visits from my mother remind me that I am never alone. She is still very near. Just because I can't hug her, it doesn't mean she isn't there. I still talk to her every day.

As I wrote this, a small white butterfly was perched on my windowsill.

———◆———

Anne Bardsley, editor of Angel Bumps, *is a humor and sentimental writer. She has been married for thirty nine years to her "wrinkle maker" husband.She has five grown children and four beautiful grandchildren who keep her young. Her first book was* How I Earned My Wrinkles...Musings on Marriage, Motherhood and Menopause. *She's been featured on Erma Bombeck, Better after 50, Purple Clover, Paradise News, Very Funny Women, Island Reporter, Feisty After Fifty, Midlife Menopause, The Grand Magazine and many others. She blogs on her website www.annebardsley.com.*

She lives in St Pete, FL.

A Mystical Rose

GAIL COLLINS

They say that the worst thing that can happen to a parent is losing a child. I can attest to that after seeing the grief that washed over my brother Tom, and his ex-wife Nancie, when they lost their only daughter. Keeley was sixteen when she died instantly in a car accident. Her family and friends, who love Keeley, will never get over losing her too soon. She truly has touched our lives in a deep and special way.

God is with us even though He seems miles away, alienated from the situations in your life. I think of the poem "Footprints in the Sand". There are certain times in my life when God has literally carried me. The day Keeley died was one of them.

The day after Keeley was killed, I picked up my rosary beads and went into a room alone to pray. I didn't know what else to do. I'd never known a sadness this deep. I asked God the age old questions that everyone asks,

"Why, God, why? She was so young and fresh. Why did her life get cut off in such a short time span?"

When Keeley had visited our house, you could hear the laughter before you reached the door. She loved her Grandmom and Grandpop. She loved us all! Now we were lost without her.

Just yesterday, it seemed, she was so excited, laughing, and experiencing life through her teenage years. She was looking forward to going to the New Jersey beaches that summer, learning how to drive, graduating from high school; all the dreams teenagers have.

I only asked God for one request. I told no one else about it. This was between me and God. "Please, God, send us a single red rose to let me know that Keeley is okay in Heaven." I was thinking of a physical rose, as most humans would. I looked everywhere for my rose sign. He sent a mystical rose instead.

After God helped us through the funeral, everything was a blur... I forgot about my request for a sign. At the end of that week, my brother Mike called me. He said, "I keep having a vision of Keeley in a field. She's wearing a white dress. She has a big smile on her face. Her hair is blowing in the wind. She looks so happy."

Then I remembered my request to God. Why hadn't He sent me my sign?

I admit I was a bit upset with God. Within a few seconds, my brother added, "Oh I forgot to tell you. Her hand was outstretched and she was holding a red rose."

I was ecstatic! I never thought God would have answered my prayers the way He did, allowing Keeley to deliver the message herself. God does answer prayers in visions and dreams. Thank you, God. You are blessed with a new angel in Heaven.

———◆———

Gail Collins lives in Lancaster, Pennsylvania. She is an avid shopper and collector of fine things. Her two pups keep her entertained. She enjoys travel, sunsets on St Pete Beach, and a glass of wine with friends.

A Window of Light
Lola Di Giulio De Maci

I had three children. Two live with me here on earth, and one lives with God in heaven. But wherever they are, they are my children—all three—and I love them.

When I was thirty-seven years old, I had my third and last child—a baby daughter. She tiptoed into my life on a warm August evening and then left as quickly as she had come, seeing the light of only one morning. She was nine hours and one minute old. But in my heart, she had lived a lifetime and a day. In the days that followed, it was hard for me to see anything through my tears. I was heartbroken and devastated. I didn't know if I would make it.

But one Sunday morning, a few months later, something strange and wonderful happened. I was sitting in my family room looking out at boxes of red geraniums I had just planted when an exceptionally bright beam of light flashed across the sliding glass door. The light quickly bolted toward the back of the kitchen, leaving me breathless.

Without hesitation, I got up from the couch and followed it. The light had settled in the center of the kitchen window, appearing in the form of a beautiful dove, its perfectly sculpted wings painted with sunlight. Awestruck, I called for my seven-year-old daughter and four-year-old son. I wanted to share this moment with them.

"Hurry!" I called out. "Hurry! Come see the beautiful white bird!"

They scampered down the hallway and into the kitchen where the brilliant rays from the dove warmed the room. My little son grabbed my hand, his eyes fixed on the window. This unexpected Sunday visitor softly fluttered its wings, as if wanting to come in.

"Let's let it in, Mamma!" my daughter cried.

"How will we get it back outside again?" I said, not knowing what to do. "Maybe it wants to be free."

Where did this bird come from? I wondered. Why was it at my window? Had it seen my tears? Did it have a message for me?

We stood there bathed in this circle of light, totally caught up in this dove's presence. Ribbons of peace and joy and contentment enveloped me. I gently embraced my children, grateful for their presence in my life. And for a moment, I felt like everything was right with the world... like all three of my children were standing there with me. All three. My heart was full.

And then the light seemed to disappear as quickly and miraculously as it had appeared. I didn't see the dove fly away. It was there... and then it wasn't. It had simply slipped away, blending quietly into the morning sun.

The following day, I dropped my daughter off at her second-grade classroom. I told my daughter's teacher, Sister Roberta, what we had seen. She listened to my story as if every word were a prayer, serenity gathering in the neatly-pressed folds of her veil. She was convinced that this magnificent white bird was the soul of my baby daughter coming back to earth to thank me for giving her eternal life. What a beautiful sentiment, I remembered thinking. And what's more... I believed her.

———◆———

Lola Di Giulio De Maci is a retired teacher whose stories have appeared in numerous editions of Chicken Soup for the Soul, *the Los Angeles Times, Sasee and Reminisce magazines, as well as other publications. Lola has a Master of Arts in education and English. She writes from her loft overlooking the San Bernardino Mountains.*

An Angel in a Cabriolet

Anne Bardsley

Some signs are unique, just like the person who sends them.

Stephanie's sign was not only unique; it brought smiles, tears, and laughter to her mom, all at the same time. That would be just like her.

The day Stephanie turned fifteen, she began to search for the car she wanted for her sixteenth birthday. She dreamed of the day she'd get her license. Stephanie talked incessantly about this car. It had to be a convertible. It had to be purple. Most importantly, it had to be a Volkswagen Cabriolet. She hoped that one would arrive for her sixteenth birthday.

Unfortunately, Stephanie went to Heaven before her car arrived. Her family was devastated. She was such a light in their lives. No parent should ever have to go through this heartbreak.

I never met Stephanie, but friends have described her as a charmer with a great sense of humor. She was an athlete. She played on the varsity basketball team, continuing the family tradition. She was loved not only by her teammates, but the entire school. To this day, the school offers a scholarship in her name.

I was in a women's group with her mom and six other women. We called ourselves the Bridge Club, but we didn't play bridge. We were more of a virtual bridge. We supported each other as we crossed our bridges in life.

I'd experienced signs from my dad when he passed. When I shared his signs with the group, Regina wondered why Stephanie hadn't sent her a sign. I wondered myself. Surely, she was sending a sign to her mom, dad, and brother. They must be missing it, I thought to myself.

The following month, we had a getaway girls retreat at the New Jersey shore. One of the gal's parents had a beautiful home on the bay. I thought for sure a dolphin would pop up in the water and chirp at Regina, as a sign. No dolphin appeared. I wanted a sign to appear for her so badly. She missed Stephanie. She was her only daughter and they were inseparable, until now. I couldn't even imagine the depths of that sadness.

Conversations about signs came up a few times that weekend. Regina was upset that she hadn't received her sign. "She knows how much I love her. Why won't she send me a sign?" I began to wish I never mentioned signs. I felt so sad that she hadn't received one.

The weekend flew by and on Sunday we drove home in pairs. Regina drove and Kathy rode shotgun in the same car. As they made the drive on the NJ Turnpike, a car kept passing them. It would slow down, so Regina could pass and then it sped up again to pass her. It was a cat and mouse ride for the two-hour ride home. Regina was annoyed to say the least. They were discussing signs again, "I really don't know why she hasn't send me something so I know she's alright. I miss her so much!" Kathy assured her that sooner or later, she would get her sign.

"What is wrong with that driver? That car has passed me the entire ride. Then it slows down and after I pass, it passes me again. That driver is playing some sort of game with us," she moaned. "Seriously, I am not in the mood for this."

The conversation continued. "So you really think she will definitely send me a sign?"

They stopped to pay the toll as they reached their home exit.

Kathy had a big grin on her face. "Look, there's your sign!" she cried. Next to them was that annoying driver in a brand new, purple, convertible, Volkswagen Cabriolet. A young girl with long, brown hair smiled at them and drove away.

Message received, Stephanie.

Angel on the Soccer Field

Desiree Moran Fray

It was perfectly understandable that my mom would visit me at my daughter's soccer tournament. She'd spent half her life as a pioneer for women's soccer. When my brother and I played in high school, she was outraged that boys playing soccer had more opportunities than the girls. Her mission became leveling the field; in this case, the soccer field.

My mom began to get involved as a team manager through roles at regional and national levels. In addition to her leadership roles at the state level, she served on the US Youth Soccer Olympic Program.

The National League for 'girls' soccer didn't even exist when she began her mission. Previously there wasn't enough draw for big cities to sponsor women's soccer tournaments. Currently, every large city sponsors events to sold-out crowds. I think my mom still attends every event, in spirit.

In 1991, the US National Women's soccer team

competed in first Women's World Cup in China. My mom was so proud. It wasn't just her dedication to the sport that got her recognition. She was a true pioneer for women. Not only did she support the players, but she supported the women coaching the girls, including the competition.

She encouraged women coaches to bring their children to the events. She even hired babysitters, so the women could coach their teams. It became a very close-knit family of women supporting not only the sport, but other women.

My mom was diagnosed with pancreatic cancer in the fall of 2007. My family and the entire women's soccer organization were devastated. Her spirits were high and her faith was strong. Her regional teams sent her personal videos of games and messages to cheer her. She loved those girls and they loved her.

Telling her, "Mom it's okay for you to go. We will miss you, but we will be alright," were the hardest few words I've ever spoken. I couldn't watch her in pain anymore and I knew in Heaven, she'd be at peace. She died a few days later, in my father's arms.

A few months ago, college coaches arrived to scout my daughter's team. I was a nervous wreck. I chewed my nails. I paced on the sidelines. My heart raced. I watched the college coaches write notes on their pads and felt even more nervous. My daughter had the potential to earn a full scholarship. I wanted her to shine on the field.

I whispered the words, "Mom, I really wish you were here with me now." I glanced across the field, and I couldn't believe my eyes. My mother was in the stands! She was right in the middle, surrounded by people. She was smiling and waving to me. Her arms were waving, as if she was saying, "I'm here! I'm here!"

I never wanted to blink or look away. My mom was with me, watching as her granddaughter scored a goal. It's hard to describe the sense of calm that filled me. I was so peaceful. I blinked and when I opened my eyes, she was gone.

So many times a coach or a player will walk up to me on the field and ask, "Are you Charlotte Moran's daughter?"

When I say, "Yes," I get a big smile and usually a hug. They tell stories of how she influenced them. There is always a personal mention of something she did that touched them.

Naturally, soccer was the main conversation, as my mom would have wanted it. She was a humble woman who never bragged about her notoriety in women's soccer.

After her death, we started The Charlotte Moran Foundation in her honor to support the girls National Soccer team. Her dream and spirit will live on in her foundation.

I know my mom is near. I talk to her all the time. My kids talk about her, and to her. They have so many good memories of their time together. God blessed them with an extra special grandmom.

When people say, "You look just like your mom," I thank them profusely. I inherited her love of Christmas tree ornaments, her sense of humor, her love of family... and of course, her love of soccer.

If I could just sit with her in the stands, I'd hold her tight and never let her go.

———— ◆ ————

Desiree Moran Fray is the mother of three teenage soccer players. She attended the University of Hartford on a soccer scholarship. She spends her time driving from state to state for soccer tournaments with her kids. She is a coffee connoisseur. She also enjoys a glass of wine with friends.

Angels at Au Bon Pain
Suzette Martinez Standring

Today I gave a young man a spirit message from his dead mother. I know, weird. I'm not a small medium at large. I'm not a psychic. It just happened.

There I was, waiting for my sandwich-soup combo, and the twenty-something-year-old behind the counter was about to hand me my food. Then he paused and looked at me as if I were a ghost.

"Are you Filipino?" he asked.

"Yes."

"I can't believe it. You look just like my mother. I had to do a double-take! You look exactly like her."

"Well, I'll take that as a compliment," I said.

"It is, but she passed away two years ago."

He handed me my order and I said, "Oh, thank you, and I'm so sorry." But he gave me a big smile.

My own mother passed away in 1987, and years later, I spotted a woman on the street who looked like her, walked like her and even wore the same fake fur hat my mom would occasionally wear. My heart caught in my throat and I wanted to run after that stranger in the street and touch her.

At Au Bon Pain, I wondered how that young man must feel to "see" his mother again. Before I could even tuck into my chicken noodle soup, I said this prayer, "Dear God, wouldn't it be nice if he could get a message from his mother? Is there something I could tell him?"

Now this is not typical. I am SO not the Long Island Medium. Maybe it was the longing in his eyes when he stared at me. Or maybe I can't leave things alone. As my sister once said, "You always have to get involved!"

Suddenly, in my mind, I saw a dress with vivid red flowers, a vibrant pattern, big blooms. Now why did I think of that? Should I ask him about it, and then take it as proof of a message to give him? I felt hesitation, doubt.

Then I felt the wash of a mother's love come over me. His mother. Surely that would be a welcome message from her spirit. Yet I started to question back in prayer, "Am I supposed to walk over to the sandwich counter and talk to him while people are in line listening? He'll think I'm a kook. Maybe this is a bad idea."

Just then he walked right past my table, another sign.

I said, "Excuse me. This is embarrassing, but I have to ask. Did your mother have a favorite dress with bright red flowers?"

He said, "She did. She was buried in it. It had big red roses up and down the dress."

I said, "Well, I was praying just now and God is allowing her spirit to give you a message. She's very, very proud of you. She loves you so much. You're about to make a big change. Are you thinking of moving away or changing jobs soon?"

His eyes got big. "I have a new job interview this afternoon."

"Well, whatever happens, she's very proud of you, and she wants you to turn to God. Pray to Him for help. Go to God."

He stared at me, silent. "That is exactly what my mother would have said. She was so religious, but I wasn't, not really. But that's OK because she never forced religion on me, but she always said to us, 'Go to God for all your problems.'"

I felt a wave of happiness and relief, looking up at him, my soup now a little cold.

He said, "Can I hug you? You don't know how you made my day!"

And on behalf of his mother, I gave him a hug. I finished my lunch, feeling a sense of wonder for the rest of my day.

———— ◆ ————

Suzette Martinez Standring is the award-winning author of The Art of Column Writing *and* The Art of Opinion Writing. *She is syndicated with GateHouse Media. Visit www. readsuzette.com.*

Bicentennial Angel

KIM DALFERES

My Grumps, my grandfather on my mother's side, left this world too soon. I know there is a big plan—a master plan—and it's not for us to question or doubt there is a reason for how it all comes together and works out. But I stand by my statement: Grumps left this world too soon.

Grumps was a gentle and kind man. He loved to drive. He drove an old, beat-up, yellow Vega, but he didn't care. Back when the price of gasoline was a non-issue, he loved to drive over to Palm Beach on Sunday afternoons after church and lunch. Even during the gas crisis of the seventies, when you had to wait in line for hours to get gas and hope that the station didn't run out before you got to the pump, he still liked to drive over to Palm Beach. Inside that little yellow car, with the windows down, we would wind back and forth along the road that travels along that stretch of beach, and we would slow down and stare at all the big mansions, peering through the gates and the tall bushes. All you could see of the Kennedy compound was a weathered wooden door. Grumps also liked to stop and park at the beach, and we would get out and sit on the sea wall and, well, just sit.

Grumps was a terrific grandpa who attended school performances and plays and back-to-school nights and occasionally stopped by the house to mow the lawn for Mom. We lived about two miles away. He got me and Scotty a dog—Louie, the deaf poodle—when he decided we needed something to take care of and love and learn to be responsible for. He was always there, in the way children take for granted that people will always be there.

He was a faithful member of the Catholic Church, and on Sundays he would reward Scotty and me for attending Mass with the occasional trip to Dunkin' Donuts. We would sit at the pink terrazzo counter and eat our glazed donuts and drink chocolate milk while Grumps had a "dunker" with his coffee. On one occasion, Scotty tried to order chili. Poor kid, he got teased about that one for a long time.

Grumps died at the end of June 1976. He was only sixty-three years old. It seemed sad to me that he would not see the bicentennial celebration on July 4th. The bicentennial was huge; it took over the U.S. and everyone was patriotic and all red, white, and blue. I still get a tiny thrill when I come across one of those bicentennial quarters in circulation. Officially, Grumps died from pancreatic cancer. However, his treatment was complicated by emphysema, caused by years of smoking. It's odd, but I don't recall ever seeing him smoke. I'm sure he did, and I vaguely remember a pipe, but I can't recall ever seeing him with a cigarette.

The day he died was tragic. Grumps would be the first person in my life I would lose. At twelve years old, I didn't really know how much that was going to affect me. My uncle came to tell my mom, and I knew it had happened even before Uncle Tommy started to talk. It was so hard for my mom. She had been divorced for five years, and I think Grumps had been helpful, caring, and supportive. I say "I think" because my mom's a private person. She doesn't talk much about such things. Although it was more than thirty-five years ago, I remember she seemed to be so close to her dad.

On the day Grumps died, I had previously promised to babysit the neighbor's baby. When the neighbor heard the news about Grumps, she offered to cancel, but for reasons I don't quite recall, I still wanted to babysit. Maybe I simply needed something normal to do. Maybe Mom was too sad. Maybe I was twelve years old and didn't fully understand the circumstances.

The neighbor's baby was named Bunky. Now, I am sure that was not his real name, but that's the only name I can remember. Babysitting Bunky was easy. Basically, you fed him a bottle, changed the diaper, put on the night shirt, and then rocked him 'til he fell asleep. He was a good baby that way; he didn't fuss much, and he was a snuggler. For a twelve-year-old, it was easy money, and I could walk to work.

The rocking chair was on the back porch, which was a sort of an enclosed Florida room with white walls, and blue and green furniture. Sitting there, rocking Bunky, I started to feel sad. I recall the TV was turned off, and it was quiet as I listened to Bunky make baby noises and drift off to sleep. Here was this little baby who had his whole life ahead of him, falling asleep in my arms, and it made me think of Grumps and his time with us being over. I started to cry and realized I wouldn't see him again, and I wondered what our lives were going to be like with him gone.

And then, right then, I felt him in the room. I can't say I saw Grumps, but I felt him, his presence, there next to me, around me, like a warm, soft blanket. I felt really peaceful and not exactly happy but kind of calm and reassured. It was like somehow knowing things were going to turn out OK. At that moment, I knew Grumps was saying goodbye and I needed to be OK with his moving on. I felt love, a real spiritual love, in the briefest of moments. I still know that feeling, even today. I looked down at Bunky, and then Grumps was gone.

That was the last time I ever saw Grumps. I never told anyone this story, not until right now. Nearly forty years have gone by, and I sometimes wonder how our lives might have been different if he had stayed here with us a little bit longer. I think he would have liked how I turned out. I know he would love his great-grandson Jimmy, and my husband Greg. I think he would have really enjoyed retirement with my grandma who lived on for another twenty-five years. I picture them vacationing and driving, always driving. Sometimes, when I'm sitting at the beach, I think about him leaning up against the sea wall. He was a good man. You would have liked him. Everybody did.

———— ◆ ————

This essay was previously published in "I Was In Love With a Short Man Once" an essay collection by Kimberly J. Dalferes. Reprinted here with permissions.

Kimberly "Kimba" Dalferes is a native Floridian who pretends to be a Virginian. She's an accomplished king salmon slayer, estate sale junkie, and sometimes writes books, including I Was In Love With a Short Man Once *and* Magic Fishing Panties. *Dalferes' essays have been featured in diverse publications, such as the* Roanoke Times, Feisty After 45, Reflections On Smith Mountain Lake, BonBon Break, Erma Bombeck Writers' Workshop, Better After 50, *and* Midlife Boulevard. *Dalferes' humor column,* Dock Tale Hour, *has been featured in* Laker Magazine *since 2014. She's also had a limerick published in the* Washington Post, *which she emphatically claims as a legitimate publication cred. You can find her hanging out in* The Middle-Aged Cheap Seats—*her blog, kimdalferes.com/blog or visit her at www.kimdalferes.com*

Bird Watching

Kathy Coulter

My father was an avid bird-watcher. After he passed away, I had several encounters with elegant hawks who would "visit" me, soar close, and show off in the wind. I knew that the appearances of these birds were Dad's way of checking in with me. I could tell by the warm feeling that engulfed me, as I watched them soar. A calm would come over me.

I knew my dad would send me a sign. He knew I'd miss him so much and he'd need to let me know he was still in my life, here on earth. I understand why hawks were my dad's favorite now. When they are soaring mid-air, with their huge wings spread, they are a breathtaking sight to behold. Being in the presence of such a majestic creature makes me feel like my dad is right beside me.

Several years after my dad passed away, my younger brother died suddenly. It was devastating to me. I often made my morning commute to work in tears, talking to him. I told him that I thought of him as being in Heaven with our dad, and that I envisioned both as proud, glorious hawks, flying free.

One morning, I was especially sad, and as I drove, I told my brother that I hoped he didn't mind me imagining him as a hawk. Moments later, my car was passed by a huge truck, bright white and shiny, with a large logo painted on the side: "Two Hawks Trucking, Inc." Part of the logo design included a line drawing of two majestic hawks flying in tandem.

The truck slowed as it passed me, and the driver and I traveled next to each other for a few minutes. Then the truck pulled ahead. I was dumbfounded at first, then very grateful for the message.

Right behind the Two Hawks truck, there was another, smaller panel truck, from a 24-hour electric and HVAC repair service. I don't remember the exact name of the company, but I do remember the logo—a big goofy-looking owl that would make anybody laugh out loud. It read, "We're night owls." Yes, it was another bird, but a dopey one ... and I just knew it was my brother, cracking a joke to make sure he got his point across. It was *so* like him.

Since that morning, I have researched the Two Hawks Trucking Company and the electric and HVAC repair service, to confirm their existence. I've had no luck. There is no hint of a business with either of those names or logos... not in the White Pages, not in the Yellow Pages, not in the Better Business Bureau, and not in Internet searches.

My brother managed a special message to me that morning—that I am not to be sad. He and our dad are both fine. And no, he doesn't mind being a hawk for me.

Kathy Coulter lives in northeast Indiana with her husband, two adult children, and one wise, expressive orange cat. She is enjoying retirement after a long teaching career, and spends time in the garden whenever possible. She is always on the lookout for hawks.

Bubble Heart
Sheryl Gambino-Nuskey

Every Christmas Eve, our family gathers together for holiday merriment and my mom and my sisters spend hours and days preparing food for a festive dinner. Sounds familiar, yes? Not so different from most homes.

My brother, John—a single dad to three children—made it his part of the family tradition to stand in front of the sink after the Christmas Eve meal, and not budge until the dishes were done and the kitchen was sparkling. It was his sweet way of thanking the ladies for a job well done.

John was sweet, but he was also a natural born prankster. He loved to torment the family, in harmless ways. I always knew when he visited our house when I wasn't home. His calling card was re-arranging my garden decorations. I'd spend hours in my garden, making sure the flowers blended and carefully placing my garden decorations. The blue gnome was always on the left, angel statue on the right, the bicycle spin wheel was in the center. I balanced out the other décor. Then John would arrive and remove certain ones.

He knew I was a garden fanatic and I'd see that something wasn't just right. He thought tormenting his sister was hysterical.

Several years after John's passing, on Christmas Eve, the sink was piled high with dishes. As my sisters and I stood there, thinking of my brother, we noticed a perfectly-formed, heart-shaped drop of water glistening back at us—just where John would have been standing and happily cleaning the messy dishes.

Unlike most bubbles, it didn't pop. It stayed on the counter, until we returned with our cameras. Without thinking, we started to clear the dishes before taking any photos, because who wants to have a sink full of dirty dishes in their pictures? That's when we realized.... we did! We couldn't tell the story without showing the mess that John would have taken care of for us, had he been there.

The bubble remained after the dishes were gone. We talked about how much we missed his big smile and his goofy pranks.

Our teardrops fell without leaving much of a mark on the swirling bubbles of detergent in the sink, but the heart-shaped drop of water left a huge mark on our hearts.

Our brother joined us in his own special way that Christmas Eve. Then the bubble popped on its own.

Sometimes a sink full of dishes can equal hearts full of love.

———◆———

By day, Sheryl Gambino-Nuskey is the Cake Artist/Owner of Sugar Buzz, living in Pennsylvania, creating custom cake designs. By night, she is a blog reader/writer and internet marketing researcher. Day and night, she happily spends her free time with her husband, their three children/spouses and their nine grandchildren.

Find her online and learn more about her at www.sugarbuzz.co (save the m for mmmmm), www.facebook.com/sugarbuzzbakery and www.instagram.com/sugar_sheryl.

Call from a Medium

Anne Bardsley

I thought I could handle it. It was the first anniversary of my mom's passing. I didn't want to sit around and cry all day. I thought if I went to my gift shop, I'd stay busy and I could get through the day without tears. To be certain of a distraction, I brought a big wicker basket with four of our kittens who were ready for a good home.

My store was "Anne's House of Angels...Gifts From the Heart." The store was filled with angels and gifts to touch one's heart. Years prior, I'd had a visit from two angels and it changed my life. I wanted to pass along the peace and love that came to me during that visit.

I made a sign that read *Free Angelic Kittens.* The kittens wandered the store. One minute they were climbing on a rocking chair that held singing angel bears and the next, they fell asleep in the basket. No tissues were needed. The kittens were the perfect distraction. I hadn't shed a tear. One by one the kittens were taken. There was just one little gray female left when a neighbor shop owner came by to visit. She held the kitten, stroking her as the kitten curled into her arm.

"Do you think she'll miss her mom?" she asked innocently.

She did not just say that!

My heart exploded. The floodgates opened. I was sobbing as I rang up purchases. One customer made a comment, "You must really hate to see that kitten leave." He had no idea that it was my mom I missed. "I've never seen such a cat lover in my life," he continued. This happened at two in the afternoon. I cried until five o'clock and all the way home too.

Whatever made me think that I could block such sadness by working? How strong do I think I am? It was insanity. I would never suggest that to another person in my life. I couldn't even tell anyone the real reason for my tears. Every time I tried to explain, the sadness got deeper and my tears came harder.

I inherited my work ethic from my mom. She worked through every issue in her life. I come from ridiculous work genes. There was always work to be done.

My mom would have told me, "Get yourself together, Anne," if she'd been alive and at the store that day. She'd have given me a pat me on the back, handed me some tissues and brewed a pot of tea. There was never time to be this sad.

The strange thing is a few days later, one of the mediums who did angel readings at the store called me. She said, "This is going to sound very strange. I got a message from your mom this morning."

"I didn't request a reading," I told her.

"I know," she continued. "This is just a message that she asked me to deliver to you."

"Like a special delivery message?" I asked, chuckling.

"You decide," she said. "She was holding a kitten. She wants you to know you don't have to be sad. She is in a good place now. She loves you and will never leave your side." Then she asked me, "What was that about? Your mom has a kitten in Heaven?"

I laughed and I cried, explaining it all.

"That was one of the most emotional days in my life," I told her as I sniffled.

"Do you think the kitten will miss her mom?" my shop owner had asked.

I didn't know, but I sure missed mine.

Calling Them Home
Miranda Gargasz

I saw my first dead person on my sixth birthday. The woman I would forever associate with polyester, pleated pants, had died. My paternal grandmother, Maw-maw, had gone to Heaven, my mother informed me. I had only been told of her passing that morning, and I still didn't understand the finality of it all.

As I wriggled into my best dress, thoughts whirled around my head.

What was it like in Heaven?

Does it have everything Maw-maw likes?

Did they have coffee and cigarettes?

Were there Shirley Temple movies?

I walked into the living room and saw my father, a behemoth of a man, dressed in his finest clothes. He was bent over, putting on his dress shoes, and all I could see was his slicked back hair. It looked wet and I wondered if it would be hard or soft if I touched it. As I reached out my hand, he sat up, and I froze.

The giant of a man that I called "Dad," the man who struck the chord of fear in my soul with one pursed look or a simple point of a finger, was crying. Seeing his red-rimmed eyes was the first clue I had that maybe Maw-maw being in Heaven wasn't a good thing.

Before I had completely processed seeing my father cry, my mother ushered us into the car with strict instructions. "We are going somewhere very serious. There will be no running or giggling. You will sit and be quiet. There will be a lot of people there who need to talk to one another. Do not disturb them."

I held my mother's hand into the funeral home. She explained to me that this is where Maw-maw's visitation would be. My six-year-old brain processed the idea of visiting much differently than what I experienced in that room. Visiting at Maw-maw's house was a gaggle of people gathered around her kitchen table, drinking coffee, smoking cigarettes, and gossiping. There was always laughter. There was no laughter here. We entered a sea of people speaking in hushed tones, mingling. The only things visible to me were men's cuffs and ladies' waistlines.

"Mommy, where is Maw-maw?"

"She's right there. Right up front," she whispered, pointing.

My mom picked me up, walked me to the front of the room and stood next to the body. Maw-maw's face was pasty and fake-looking. She wore a dress I had never seen before. Her expression was, for lack of a better word, lifeless.

"That's not Maw-maw."

"Yes, baby, it is."

"Is she sleeping? Wake her up."

"Honey, I can't. She's dead. Her soul went to live with Jesus and God in Heaven."

"Tell her to come back," I said.

My mother began to tear up and told me the story of how our souls go to Heaven, and that this world makes us sick. God comes and saves us from the pain. Lifting me up, she told me to kiss my grandmother goodbye.

That innocent action, a cold I've never felt since, the taste of makeup on my lips, was enough to solidify my fear of death and funerals for a lifetime.

For years, I was angry with God for taking my grandmother away, for never allowing me to see her again. How could He? It seemed selfish to take her away when I was so young. I carried that hurt in my heart for decades, never forgiving Him.

Other friends and family passed away over time, and I couldn't go near their bodies. The thought of how cold they were, how they didn't look like themselves haunted me. I could still taste the makeup on my lips. Each time, I sat in the very back of the room, shaking, desperately trying to avoid an anxiety attack.

When I was thirty-six-years old, Gene, a family friend, died. I was so worried that I would freak out and embarrass myself that I waited for the entire room to fill before I entered the chapel with my husband, Jim, by my side. We sat in the very back, all the other attendees blocking my view of the body. I kept my head down and cried softly. I willed myself to stay calm.

I was fine until his sister stood to say some final words, and panic rose in my chest. I covered my mouth with tissues, trying not to sob out loud. Jim took my hand and squeezed it.

"Are you okay?" he whispered. "You can step out if you need to."

You will sit and be quiet... Do not disturb them.

I stayed put, my mother's words fully ingrained from thirty years before.

It was then that I felt a hand rub my back in a soothing manner and a wave of calm rush over my body. I instantly stopped crying and could breathe. I looked down at my lap and saw Jim's hand firmly clasped in mine. When I turned, there was no one behind me, no one beside me.

Was it Gene telling me it would be okay?

Was it Maw-maw, soothing her wounded grandchild?

Was it God, giving me peace to deal with death?

I don't have the answers. All I know is that Gene's was the first funeral I made it through without being an absolute mess by the end. I left his wake feeling like there was a process to living, that as badly as it made survivors feel, it was right that our loved ones die and go on. It was much like when we were children and our mothers called us home—there's a time for play and then there's a time for being serious.

I'd like to think some angel, whether Maw-maw, Gene, or one of God's nameless messengers was there that day, calming one of His lost sheep. That He was making it clear that death is just one stop on an eternal journey. Their lives were their play and, like our mothers, it was time that God called them Home.

———◆———

Miranda Gargasz writes Christian fiction with publishing cred-its in the Christian Science Monitor *and* Humor Press. *She currently lives in Ohio.*

Chatting with Mom
Christy Heitger-Ewing

I can't wait to tell Mom about this!

I had that thought a dozen times a day when I was in grade school. I was always so eager to rush home and tell Mom the silly stories and crazy drama from the classroom, hallway, cafeteria, and playground. I gleefully shared every detail of my day, and Mom listened intently, always offering sound advice and an enlightened perspective.

This dynamic continued between me and Mom all through high school, college, and well into adulthood. When I became a mother myself, our conversations evolved but were still filled with joy, insight, and laughter.

So, when Mom died unexpectedly, I was devastated.

With the loss of my constant chatting companion, my world fell deafeningly silent.

Stop, Look, and Listen

One day I told my minister Ben how much I missed communicating with Mom.

"Who says you have to stop?" he asked.

I furrowed my brow. "What do you mean?" "Energy never dies. It only changes form," Ben said. "I'll bet your mom will find ways to continue talking to you. You just have to be open to listening."

Though that sounded like a sweet premise for a cheesy Hallmark movie, in real life, I wasn't buying it.

"I know a lot of people claim that they can feel their loved one's presence," I said. "But I've never been able to. It's not that I don't want to. I'm *desperate* to connect, but I can't."

"You might be trying too hard," Ben noted. "Perhaps you should wait for her to come to you."

What? This wasn't a bus stop. What was I waiting for? And how long would I be left hanging? I was frustrated and irritable. Antsy and agitated. Ticked off and torn up.

Besides, I wasn't the passive type, content to sit back and wait for Mom's energy to visit me in the form of a butterfly or whatever. And even if she did, what kind of meaningful conversation was I going to have with an insect?

Nevertheless, despite my skepticism, I prayed to get some sort of "sign" that would show me that my mom was still with me in spirit.

A MESSAGE FROM MOM

The next day Dad shared an interesting story with me. He, too, had been struggling with Mom's loss. After nearly 50 years together, he didn't know how to begin to move forward and live a life without my mom in it, so he spoke out loud to her constantly but was always met with silence.

Dad told me that he had been hunting for stamps in

his desk when a greeting card fell out of a cubby hole and landed on the floor by his feet.

Though the card had not been made out to anyone, it was clearly meant for Dad's eyes.

The message said, "I believe in faith and prayers and angels that watch over us. I believe in amazing grace and miracles that happen where we least expect to find them. I believe in new days that bring new beginnings. I believe in a God who wants only the best and brightest for you always."

Dad felt both heard and healed now that he had an idea of what Mom wanted for him.

While I was happy that Mom had communicated with Dad, I must admit that I was a little jealous. What about me? Where was my sign from heaven?

ANGEL ON A PARK BENCH

Several weeks later, on an overcast day, I took my two-year-old son Trevyn to the local park. I hadn't been there much since Mom's passing because it was a tough place to go. I often saw proud grandmothers watching their precious grandbabies swing, climb, and slide. And every time I heard one of the children shout, "Watch me, Gamma!" my breath caught in my throat because that used to be my mom—a happy, devoted grandmother who would do anything to make her grandchildren smile. Now she was gone, and the sting of sadness pierced me.

"Mama!" Trevyn called to me as he stood beside a plastic captain's wheel attached to the play set. "Look! Boat!"

Trevyn pretended to pilot his vessel while I took a seat on an adjacent wooden bench. I scanned the area and spotted a mom's group on the opposite end of the park. The women were gathered around a picnic table preparing lunch while their kids played tag. As I watched the mothers laughing, chatting, and doling out chocolate chip muffins, an intense wave of loneliness washed over me.

That used to be my life, I thought. *A life full of laughter, joy, and conversation.*

Out of the corner of my eye, I noticed that my son was tossing wood chips high into the air.

"Trevyn!" I called out. "No, no, sweetie."

He went back to his captain's wheel. Meanwhile, I sat with my hands folded loosely in my lap, studying my spotted, freckled hands. They looked just like Mom's, weathered from all the hours she had spent in the garden as a youth. I thought about how much Mom and I had in common besides our sun-damaged skin. We both had dark brown eyes, super soft hair, a high-pitched giggle, and a dreadfully poor sense of direction.

My mind wandered back to the crisp fall day when she and I had gone wedding dress shopping. We had the windows rolled down in the Honda Accord and were so busy gabbing, singing, and laughing as the wind blew through our hair that we drove 60 miles out of our way. I chuckled at the bittersweet memory as a single tear rolled down my cheek.

MY RED-HEADED BUTTERFLY

I glanced up to check on Trevyn and noticed a little red-headed girl making a beeline for me. She looked to be Trevyn's age, maybe a bit older.

"Can I sit wiff you?" she asked.

"Sure," I said, scooching down a bit to make room. She struggled to climb onto the bench because in her right hand she held the bottom portion of a half-eaten chocolate chip muffin.

From across the playground, the little girl's mom called out, "Honey, come back here!"

But Muffin Girl didn't budge. Still holding the sticky treat in her right hand, she gently placed her left hand on my forearm and looked at me with warm, empathetic eyes. Instantaneously, I felt calmed by the nurturing and watchful presence of this young stranger.

The little girl seemed to sense that I was struggling. She tenderly patted my arm with her left hand, leaned towards me, and inquired with sweet innocence, "You o-tay?"

Tears sprung to my eyes.

"Yes," I said as my heart raced with an odd but familiar energy.

"And Te-vin o-tay?"

My eyebrows shot up. She asked about Trevyn!

I realize that she had probably heard me call out my son's name a few minutes earlier, but the fact that she remembered his name and went on to ask about his well-being—those details could not be discounted.

"Yes," I replied. "Trevyn's good."

A genuine smile crossed my lips for the first time in months.

"I see you've eaten the top of your muffin," I remarked.

"Uh-huh," the girl replied with a giggle.

"I don't blame you," I said. "That's the best part."

"Yeah."

With that, she hopped down and trotted over to the playground equipment to join her friends.

A ray of sunshine peeked out from behind a thick wall of clouds. Warmth penetrated my skin as peace settled into my soul. I sat perfectly still, closed my eyes, and tilted my head back to fully absorb the warmth of the one bright beam of light cast down from overhead. It was as if Mom was offering me one of her comforting hugs.

This feeling reminded me of the days when I used to rush home from grade school with an exciting tale to tell Mom.

Trevyn called out, "Mommy," and as I took his soft, tiny hand in mind, I heard a stray squeal, clapping hands, and a flurry of giggles.

My world no longer sounded so quiet now that the chatting had resumed.

———— ✦ ————

Christy Heitger-Ewing is an award-winning writer and columnist who writes human interest stories for national, regional, and local magazines. She has contributed to a dozen anthologies and is the author of the book Cabin Glory: Amusing Tales of Time Spent at the Family Retreat *(www.cabinglory.com). Christy lives in Avon, Indiana, with her husband, two sons, and two cats.*

Christmas Ornaments

MEG HACHMAN

My dad—who passed in 1993—loved Christmas, and our family always celebrated the holiday with much joy. The centerpiece of our celebration was the Christmas tree, and the highlight of the season was the placement of the glass ornaments that my father had bought in Germany during his time in the service. He always said that German glass ornaments were the most beautiful, and over the years, he acquired many more of them. No one could touch them but him.

His favorite was a softball size, hand blown ornament with a skier in red ski pants, knees bent skiing in the snow. This ornament was fifty years old when I was a kid. It's almost a hundred years old now.

Another favorite is a snowman with a huge smile and bright orange carrot as a nose. The ball itself is gold with specks of white falling snow. The colors are still bright as new.

Each year as Mom and I hold these ornaments in our hands, I can feel my dad swell with pride that we're carrying on the appreciation of his collection. They are irreplaceable.

Ever since my father's death, my mom has carefully put up the tree with all his precious, delicate glass ornaments.

So, imagine my mother's horror when she came home from work one night to find the Christmas tree lying on the floor. She was sure that all my father's beloved ornaments would be nothing but powdered glass; but to her great relief, when the tree was lifted back onto its stand, every single ornament was still intact. We don't know how it happened, but it's true—my dad prevented the ornaments he loved so much from breaking.

A few years after Dad died, my mom—who uses a walker to get around—was told by a psychic that there was a man beside her that kept her from falling. My mom replied, "I know my husband is still with me. He kept those ornaments from breaking, didn't he?" The psychic nodded her head and smiled.

The story comes up every Christmas—a little reminder of Dad's love for us.

———— ◆ ————

Meg Hachman is a former 911 operator, retired from the city of Akron. She's been married for twenty-eight years. She has two children. She was a theatre major in college at the University of Akron where she produced many plays. She blogs at Meg on the Go (icyfar582.blogspot.com). She is working on a book about her dispatch experiences.

Dad's Snapshot

MERYL BAER

I was sorting through some cartons I'd rescued from my childhood home, when a picture unexpectedly popped up in a box of old photos and made me smile.

I was just a little girl in the picture, only four or five years old. My light brown hair was straight and pulled back off my face; I had bright blue-green eyes, pursed lips, and an almost serious expression. As a mature woman, it was hard to remember much about that child. The picture captured me at a moment in time before the problems of adolescence had begun taking their toll on me—before pimples, before boobs, before concerns about body weight, before best friends moved away, before math class made me cry. My confidence started drifting downhill as my age increased.

My dad, the family photographer and jokester, was undoubtedly the one behind the camera. And was that a cigarette in my hand? Maybe a chocolate one. Faux cigarettes made of chocolate were popular treats in the '50s.

Not to mention the fact that Dad had snapped the photo years before the Surgeon General's report on the evils of smoking.

I examined the picture closely, and saw that that the cigarette might be just a rolled-up piece of paper. I'd probably been fooling around, attempting to look hip and cool. Neither of those two words "hip" or "cool"—would ever have been used by a child so young, and yet they perfectly describe the mood I clearly attempted to convey.

I was wearing a pink blouse in the photo, and a navy-blue jacket with a red border and embroidered flowers. I looked like a cross between a tentative child and a know-it-all teen, as I sat there eyeing my dad, who'd been a chain smoker. Clearly, he'd thought the pose cute and captured it, allowing me to resurrect the occasion decades later.

Mom would throw most of the pictures, however, into a box on top of a lot of other photos, mentioning her desire to eventually go through them and make albums. But over the years the pile just got bigger, and eventually, it became mine.

I put the picture of me and my faux cigarette aside, intent on finding a small frame for it. And that's when I noticed a bag of goodies for my grandkids sitting on the coffee table. I'd purchased the treats at an old-fashioned general store on a recent trip to Hot Springs, Arkansas.

As I reached for the bag, it opened and a small rectangular box fell out. I picked it up, inspected it, and smiled. Through the clear plastic cover, I could see three chocolate cigars snuggled inside.

Thanks, Dad, for the memories.

———————— ◆ ————————

Once upon a time Meryl Baer worked for a financial firm in a strait-laced, crazy-in-its-own way kind of world. After many years she quit her job and moved to the New Jersey shore. She boasts a wonderful husband, two sons, two daughters-in-law, five grandkids, assorted relatives, and friends. All make their way to her door at the shore during the summer. No one visits in winter, so she writes. Topics include her travels and travails, family, food— definitely a favorite passion and pastime— and anything else she finds interesting. Check out her blog Six Decades and Counting: *sixdecadesandcounting.blogspot.com*.

Dialing from Heaven
Pat Rombyer

My mother was a lifelong believer in the after-life. Not only was she a devout Christian, but her views also were impacted by an old book, *Unobstructed Universe* written by Stewart Edward White.

It's the story of our potential to bridge the gap of consciousness and become alive and alert in the fullness of our being. Another of White's books, *Across the Unknown*, explains how the inner life is alive in each one of us, even while we are immersed in the physical plane. It also shows us how to tap the reality of this inner life to enrich our own.

I hadn't read the book yet, but my mother was convinced, beyond a doubt, that life goes on. I believe it had something to do with the human body's electrical impulses.

My mom was my biggest supporter. After having three sons, she was so happy to have a daughter. But I surely was a disappointment for a mom who wanted a girly girl to dress up. With three older brothers, I was a tomboy through and through.

After high school graduation, I got married and started to raise our family in Michigan. Mom moved to Florida, but every summer and Christmas, she flew home to stay with my family. I loved being able to sleep in while she was visiting and waking up to hear her and my kids making Play-Doh figures at the kitchen table, or drawing pictures or playing hangman. She was great grandmother.

Even though she lived in Florida, we spoke on the phone every Sunday night at 6:00 p.m.

We'd catch up on the weekly happenings and share stories. I could not have asked for a more supportive mother. She always seemed amazed and happy that I had turned into a decent cook and a capable mother. How could I not, with a mom like I had?

So when she died in 2007 at the age of 89, I knew if there was a way, she would communicate with me. I was with her when she died the evening of October 9 in Sarasota, Florida. Her death was not unexpected after her 12-day hospitalization, but my brother and I left feeling bereft.

Upon awakening in her bedroom the next morning, I found ALL the clock faces flashing! I smiled. She'd sent me a sign via electrical impulses.

Weeks later, back in Michigan, I was at home on a Sunday. I noticed the time was 6:00 p.m., the time my mom usually called me. In my grief, I wailed "I want to talk to my mom!" It was one of those simple things that I'd taken for granted. Now I'd give anything to talk to her one more time.

Just seconds later the phone rang and an electronic

voice said something like, "That number is no longer in service." I was stunned, but I knew. Once again, she'd sent me a message.

A year or so after her death, I was at her credit union in Sarasota, closing out her accounts. The woman behind the desk was asking the usual questions in such a kindly manner that I was holding back tears during this one more post-death thing I had to do.

As I thanked her and gathered the paperwork, she looked at me and said, "Your mother was my high school teacher. She was the best teacher I ever had." Those words triggered my tears. I couldn't contain myself. I left with tears streaming down my face. My mom touched so many lives.

I know now that she is still with me and will watch over me always. After all, we have a great connection now.

———— ◆ ————

Pat Rombyer is a retired news reporter of thirty years for the Jackson Citizen Patriot in Michigan. She's the mother of seven children and the grandmother of seven grandchildren.

She is a widow and lives with two dogs and a cat in the country, just outside of Jackson, Michigan. She fills her time volunteering, exploring genealogy, and loving life. She is not afraid of death.

Dot's Feathered Boa

Anne Bardsley

Aunt Dot, my mom's younger sister, was a spirited lady. She moved in with my mom after my dad passed away. They were both in their sixties and together they were the Laverne and Shirley of the neighborhood. When new neighbors moved into the other half of my mom's twin home, my mom and aunt were invited to a housewarming party. Naturally, they were excited to know the nice new gentleman neighbors.

When they arrived, they were surprised to find a house full of transvestite men dressed in outfits that might be worn in a Broadway play. This wasn't a "coming out" party. It was a "moving in" party. There was enough silk in the house to put a silkworm to shame. Vibrant color shirts, vests, and even silk pants and skirts were the attire. Most of them wore a feathered boa.

When Mom and Dot came for dinner, I asked about the party. They both lit up smiling and laughing. "Anne, your father would have rolled in his grave if he saw me dancing with that young man."

Dot agreed. "It was the best party of my life. Anthony wrapped a pink boa around my neck. Every hour a different color joined the pink one. I had four all together. I felt like a rainbow. We were the belles of the ball that night, weren't we, Bette?"

Mom said, "I haven't danced that much since my niece's wedding. I only had three boas, so Dot wins."

I didn't connect any of it at the time, but a feather became Dot's sign.

I was with my future daughter-in-law picking out a wedding dress when I got the call that Dot had passed. I was so sad. She was my godmother. I tried not to cry through the fittings, but it was so surreal; a happy, new life beginning and one just ended. The bridal gown was chosen and we moved on to look at dresses for the moms. That is when I backed into a full rack of multi-color feathered boas. As I wrapped the white boa around me, a feather got loose and stuck to my cheek. I dismissed it. It never registered with me.

I was driving home and I wondered what Dot's sign would be. Then I remembered the story of the party and how she loved the feathered boas. I'd almost knocked the entire rack of boas over at the store. Her sign was so obvious now.

A few months later, my sister called to say, "Aunt Dot must have been watching over Jacqui.

"Do you remember when she watched her when she was little?"

"Of course," I told her. "Every day she had a funny story about what Jacqui said or did."

Well, there were complications and Jacqui and she had to have a C-section. During the operation, a feather fell from the ceiling in a sterile operating room."

My first question was, "How did she get into the operating room?" I don't know, but I believe she was there in spirit with Jacqui, whom she loved so much. When Jacqui's baby girl was born, I know Aunt Dot danced in Heaven.

Fran's Feather

CHARLENE SMURTHWAITE

M y mother was my best friend. As a child, I remember always wanting to be wherever she was. I often remember sitting in the hall, outside the bathroom door, making plans for her evening. I'd stretch my legs across the hall resting my feet on the opposite wall, and talk to the closed door. "What are we doing tonight? Do you want to go to W.T. Grants? Do you want to go see Aunt Helen? Can we go to Fanaro's to look at their bargain table?"

Fran just couldn't shake me.

As an adult, I spoke to her almost every day. If I was going shopping and asked her to go, she'd always say, "Let me get my shoes on." If I was debating about whether to buy something in a catalog, I'd call to get her opinion. Quite often she'd say, "Get it. I'll pay half." We were like the Best Friend necklaces that fit together to make one heart.

I have two sons with autism, and Fran loved them

both very much. Friday nights were Bryan and Fran's time together. They'd go to the mall, the arcade, and out to dinner at the Apple Dumpling Diner. He still repeats things she told him; things I didn't realize they talked about. Their bond was irreplaceable.

Eric was more difficult for Fran to keep up with. She was never one to back down from a challenge, and always tried to help me with him.

One day I came home and she warned, "Don't go in there. Get yourself a cup of coffee, sit down, and watch Oprah with me. We'll deal with him later." I wondered how bad it could be, while happy sounds emanated from the room down the hall. I had to look. As I walked down the hall, she warned me again. "Char, get your coffee and we'll deal with it later." I should have listened to her. When I opened the door, feathers billowed from the room. Eric had ripped open all of our feather pillows, and had the ceiling fan on full speed. He was in his glory.

I returned to the living room, sat down, and watched Oprah. We cleaned the room later that day, but I continued to find feathers in there for months. They'd be in the kids' hair or in with the marble maze pieces. I'd get a book off the shelf, and a little puff of feathers would drift through the air. That would have scared most babysitters away, but not my mom.

Life with the boys wasn't ever easy, but my mother always helped me. It was just who she was. She could have written the book on how to be a wonderful grandparent for autistic children. She was blessed with such a good sense of humor; which always helped. Fran never tired of telling relatives stories about the boys. The feather fiasco was always her favorite and most animated story. She was so proud of them, in spite of all their pranks.

We found out that Fran had leukemia in April of 2001, and she passed away in June. It was such a horrible loss. I'd pick up the phone to call her, and remember that she was gone. I got a letter from a nurse at Fox Chase, telling me how much she thought of my mother in the short time she'd known her. She said my mother wanted to live for me and my sons.

It has been many years since Eric's feather pillow incident, but I have never forgotten that day. I continue to find feathers in the darndest places. And when I do, I think of Fran. Just maybe, she is trying to support me with these little signs. I'm guessing that things are too good in Heaven for her to be bothered with every detail of our lives, but whenever a feather appears, I feel her with me.

One of my cousins, unaware of my love of feathers, gave me a pin with the Legend of the Feather attached. There is a Legend of the Feather by Francis J Wilson, states a feather is sent from up above as a reminder of God's love. It's believed that it fell out in the struggle as your guardian angel protected you from harm.

I believe my mom was my angel on earth. She continues to watch over me, sending me feathers as her sign of protection and love.

———— ✦ ————

Charlene Smurthwaite is the mother of two autistic sons. She is an advocate for autistic children. She is constantly on the go and quite amazingly, she never complains. She is one amazing lady!

Giving a Hoot

Lee Gaitan

I'm not what you'd call a nature girl. While I appreciate the beauty of the natural world, I feel no need to camp out in it or get parts of it directly on me. A "back-to-nature" retreat to me means having fresh-cut flowers on the table beside my soaking tub. My older sister, while quite the accomplished soaker herself, was also comfortably at home in the wild. She was the child who lay in the grass and talked to the ants as they crawled up her arm, the one who gently carried every daddy longlegs from the high-traffic porch steps to the safety of the back yard.

As an adult, she regularly invited a possum into her kitchen to dine with her cats and allowed a squirrel to give birth in the hole for her dryer vent, giving the squirrel family unrestricted access to her entire house. Boy, did the realtor earn his money the day Mrs. Squirrel casually sauntered down the stairs while he was showing the place to potential buyers.

By contrast, I once paid $2,000 to evict a band of free-loading squirrels from my attic where they'd chomped their way through ten inches of insulation to lay in a supply of acorns and assorted other nuts between my rafters. It was like a Golden Corral buffet for tree rodents up there and they weren't paying me one single cent in rent.

Unlike my sister's, my encounters with undomesticated animals have traditionally not gone well. Over the years, I've been stalked by a possum, intimidated by a raccoon and head-pecked by a deranged blackbird. Back in my teenage days, the creatures that terrified me most were owls, with their weirdly human-like eyes that seemed to stare right through you. I found them so creepy I wouldn't even eat Wise potato chips. My sister, of course, thought owls fascinating, weird eyeballs and all. (But, seriously, how could I not fear something capable of spinning its head around almost 360 degrees? At 16, the only other living thing I'd seen do that was Linda Blair and we all know what was going on there!)

To my sister's great amusement, she was able to witness my fear of owls literally reach new heights one summer night when my boyfriend dropped me off from a date. She was watching from the side patio as I ran to the front door, accidentally brushing against a low-lying tree branch on my way. Instantly, a shrill, hideous screech of "Hoooooooooooo!" pierced the still night air, launching me several feet into that same air and causing me to let out a pretty hideous screech of my own.

It's hard to say which reaction was strongest, my panic, the owl's annoyance, or my sister's delight. This incident gave my sister even more ammunition for teasing "scaredy cat" me. From that point on, she missed no opportunity to sneak up on me and "hoot" and was particularly fond of doing this in darkened rooms or when I was in the shower. All these years later my left shin still bears a small scar from a hoot-induced leg-shaving mishap. As I pressed a wad of tissues against my razor cut that night, I could never have imagined the bittersweet significance a hoot would ultimately hold in my life.

At the much too young age of 43, my sister received the devastating diagnosis of early onset Parkinson's disease. For the next 22 years, she faced her diagnosis as she did everything in life, fearlessly and with great humor. She had several good years, and with a few concessions to her illness here and there we continued to have wonderful adventures together. Eventually, however, positive affirmations and a sassy attitude were no match for her cruel and merciless enemy. The last year of her life was a series of medical crises, each leaving her increasingly fragile and largely unable to move or communicate.

Early one morning last October, a strange noise invaded my sound sleep and wakened me at precisely 5:30 in the morning. It was an eerie sound, one I couldn't quite place. I listened for a few moments, but hearing nothing more, decided I must have either imagined or dreamed it. I was about to fall back asleep when a clear and mournful "hooooo" outside my window broke the predawn quiet. In nine years of living in my house I had never once heard an owl hoot. I would not only have remembered if I had, I would have probably packed my bags on the spot. With a mounting sense of dread, I sat up in bed and stared at the phone, certain the call I'd feared for the past year would come any minute. I stared at the phone for two hours until it was time to get ready for work.

In the bright light of day, my notion that the "hoot" had been a message from my sister seemed almost silly. I was chiding myself for my superstitions when the phone rang at 8:15 with the news that my sister had suffered another stroke, this one even more severe than the last, and that any minute might well be her last. Just before I hung up the phone, I asked when the stroke had occurred. 5:30 a.m. was the answer.

Stubborn to the very end, insistent on meeting death on her own terms, my sister defied her doctors' pronouncements and held on for another week, long enough for us to share a last goodbye and even a final weak smile at an old joke. And then, with barely a whimper, she was gone, taking with her a large piece of my heart.

The first night after she was gone, my sense of loss was so profound, my grief so crushing, I could do little more than crawl into bed, face unwashed, teeth unbrushed. I lay in the dark, pillow clutched to my chest, and cried for hours. Mercifully, exhaustion at last took over and I felt my eyelids getting heavy. And just as I was drifting off, I heard it. It was soft at first and then strong and clear, an unmistakable series of hoots outside my bedroom window. I sat up and listened intently for the next several minutes, but only silence followed. I lay back down and closed my eyes. Despite my sadness, despite the tears rolling down my cheeks, I couldn't help but smile. Fly high and free, my dear sister, far from the pain and limitations of this earthly realm. And thank you for giving a hoot one last time.

Lee Gaitan Note: I had originally intended to post this piece two weeks ago as a tribute to my sister on the one-year anniversary of her passing, but in the ironic circle of life, my daughter went into labor with my first grandchild during the same week. One light is extinguished and another is lit. And in honor of both, we carry on.

Lee Gaitan has worn many hats in her 25 years in communications, from public relations writer and television host to stand-up comedienne and educator. She has written two books, Falling Flesh Just Ahead, *and the Amazon #1 bestseller* My Pineapples Went to Houston—Finding the Humor in My Dashed Hopes, Broken Dreams and Plans Gone Outrageously Awry. *She has also authored chapters in the bestselling books,* The Divinity of Dogs *and* Feisty After 45. *Her work has been featured on the* Huffington Post, Erma Bombeck Humor Writers' Workshop, The Good Men Project, Mothers Always Write, *and* Sixty and Me among others. *She lives in Atlanta with her husband and dog.*

Grandpa Jay's Batteries
Anne Bardsley

There are moments that I tuck away when I meet someone special. I had one of those moments with Jay. He was my daughter's father-in-law. His head was bald. He wore dark-rimmed glasses and he sported a pair of striped suspenders. His smile lit up the room. He was a very likeable man with a gentle spirit.

My grandson Arlo was four days old when he came home from the hospital nursery. His grandpop, Jay, was holding him nestled like a football in his arms. He began to sing his own lullaby to the six-pound baby in his arms. Arlo's eyes were wide as he stared at his grandpa, mesmerized by his alto crooning. I should have snapped that picture because Jay passed away just a few months later.

Jay was always prepared. He had a compulsion to collect batteries. If there was ever a storm and the lights went out, he had enough reserve for forty flashlights, fifteen clocks, and thirty-two remote controls. Every time he and his wife went shopping, he added batteries of any size to their cart. His family teased him about this obsession. He'd just grin.

After Jay passed, and Arlo grew into a toddler, he channeled Jay's fascination with batteries. Any toy that broke, he claimed, "It needs a new battery." It didn't matter if it was a wooden truck, a car, or a stuffed animal, sooner or later they all needed a new battery.

One day a talking stuffed animal stopped working and this time it really did need batteries. He and Mommy couldn't find a single battery. Arlo declared, "We need to keep batteries in this house for emergencies! This is an emergency!" I think Jay smiled in Heaven that day.

Recently, Jay's family gathered for a picnic. These are times that catch us off guard. We expect the big things to be sad, but the simple things often catch us off guard. The wit and charm of those we've lost leave a hole at the table, as well as in our hearts. They should be there. This time, Arlo mentioned at the dinner table that his truck needed batteries. "All of my toys are broken. They all need batteries," he moaned.

He continued to complain that his Arlo the dinosaur toy stopped walking right in the middle of his construction site. "His batteries died and we didn't have the right size! Now he's stuck in the boulders at my construction site." His brow was furrowed. "How can I work like this? I need a battery factory."

Later, as dessert was served, Arlo piped in, "Does anybody have any batteries at their house?" he asked. The third mention was a charm.

"Oh my gosh!" Jay's son said and then broke out in laughter. "You're just like your Grandpop."

That's when they reminisced about Jay's fascination with collecting batteries and laughter filled the air.

I don't think Jay missed that picnic at all. Someone knew he was there.

Gusty Diane

Anne Bardsley

Diane was my office manager, and I was afraid of her for years. She was brusque and short-tempered, and she had *no* problem using her "big girl" voice.

"Anne, you know I've been here for thirty years," she'd often say. "Why do you always ask other people questions and not me?" I could never tell her that she scared me. Instead, I would lie and reply, "Oh you're so busy all the time, and I don't want to interrupt you."

"Interrupt me!" she barked.

After I got to know Diane's softer side, I came to love her. Once, she gave me a "Cool Grandma" T-shirt; another time, she offered me advice on Christmas gifts for my first granddaughter. She informed me that the Elf on the Shelf was a must-have heirloom. She gave me "grandmother books" to fill in and give to my grandkids, each book passing along information like how and where I met their grandfather, what I was like as a little girl, and facts about my life.

Diane loved being a grandmother; her grandkids were her pride and joy. They called her Nandy. They visited her often. Naturally, her condo looked like a toy store. Once her three-year-old grandson hid under my desk to surprise her at work. I paged, "Diane, please come to the front desk."

Robbie giggled at my feet as he heard her get closer. He couldn't stand the suspense! He jumped out when she was still twenty feet away, running to her and jumping in her arms, "Nandy, I'm here!" he cried. She hugged him tight. Diane was a big mush with the little ones.

She was also an avid smoker, with bad lungs; but when we'd remind her of the harm she was doing to her health, she'd light up another cigarette. We finally gave up.

Diane's health deteriorated. One day, she left the office for a doctor's appointment, and she was sent to the hospital. She never came back to work.

Within two weeks, she was gone. It came as a shock to all of us. We'd known about her health issues, but no one had thought she was critically ill. Everyone in our office felt her absence dearly.

We weren't the only ones who missed her. Every Friday night, the residents of Diane's condo would gather over margaritas; it seemed fitting that her service be held in the huge lobby of her condominium complex. A margarita machine spun all night long; the tables were filled with her favorite Mexican foods. A video of her life played in a side room. As I watched it, I realized that Diane had experienced an amazing, full life that I'd known nothing about. There was so much about her that I was never aware of.

It made me miss her even more.

As the night went on, we moved out to the patio and sat around a large table. We shared Diane stories, and we laughed and cried together. The conversation just kept flowing, and I thought to myself that Diane would definitely be smiling, as she listened to each story. Her best friend, Beverly, had traveled all the way from Texas, and she regaled us with tales of their younger years and gallivanting times. They'd been friends since high school.

Suddenly, a strong gust of wind blew onto the patio. We all grabbed our glasses and held onto the tablecloth. Plastic cups and paper plates flew everywhere. The gust was hurricane force! I jokingly said, "Well, hello, Diane!"

Maybe I should have poured her a margarita!

Grandmom's at Starbucks

Rebecca Hession

I knew today was a good day. I felt it when I opened my eyes. I felt it not from the sun or the lingering full moon or the flowers that were in full bloom. I knew from inside. I knew that my life was well aligned and all the uncertainty and the questions and the wondering about things was starting to ease into a sense of peace. The struggles would remain, because life was riddled with those, but my sense of confidence and well-being had returned.

I took my daughter to her last day of school and made my way to town, ready to take on my day. I needed Starbucks time, both for the fuel and the time to plan some events of the day. I chose a Starbucks I don't visit very often, ordered my fare and looked for a place to camp for awhile. I chose a place at one of those long communal tables. I set my bag down and looked up at my table partners, a mother and child.

Not just any child. This child was angelic. Hair spun

like gold, eyes dancing and bright as the summer sun. Her mother was leaning in, engaged completely with her child; a happy morning. I could feel it.

I smiled at the sight of them. Then I looked at the child's cup and written on it was the name Elsie. I blinked and looked again. We all know that Starbucks isn't famous for getting names right on our cup. This was not a common name, Elsie. The name of my grandmother. My favorite person on the planet grandmother that I watched take her last breath. a from *Frozen* fame, but still a nice coincidence.

But I must know.

I smiled at this beautiful angel and I said, "Honey, what's your name?" And there in what now feels like slow motion she said, "Elsie" with a shy little smile to her Starbucks stranger.

My heart melted, I was covered in chills and I smiled at her mother and said, "Oh my, that's my grandmother's name." We chatted that her beautiful angel was also named after her grandmother and what a wonderful coincidence with a not so common name on this summer morning.

I leaned down and said to little Elsie, "That's a beautiful name, honey, you must have a big heart because everyone I've ever known named Elsie has an amazingly big heart."

I returned to the counter, retrieved my drink, still a little shaken and covered in chills. As I passed by little Elsie I couldn't resist knowing more so I persisted. "Honey, what is your middle name?" And in the tiny voice of a preschooler she said, "Rose". And now I was unable to speak. I surely must not have heard her correctly so I asked one more time and she confirmed. Elsie Rose. My grandmother's **exact** name.

My tears welled and the mom's eyes got soft. Thankfully she wasn't afraid of this stranger who had now completely inserted herself into their morning. I told the mom that my grandmother was a huge part of my life and I was with her at the end and delivered her eulogy that so many have read and how it always made me feel like I have honored her well. The mom was wonderful and kind and let me have my amazing moment with her daughter. And I was grateful to be in public because I found a way to swallow the sobbing that had risen in my throat.

So today was a really, good day. It's a day of knowing and assurance and love and protection. My angels are all in place, with Grandma taking the lead.

To read her eugogy: www.randomthoughtsbyrebecca. com/2011/06/grandmas-eulogy.html#.VW73Noao4mE

Rebecca Hession writes a personal blog at www.RandomThoughtsbyRebecca.com. She is also working on a book and online training about relationships with those with Attention Deficit Disorder called Not Wrong Just Different. *Rebecca has spent the last 16 years helping her corporate clients enable greatness in leadership and productivity at Franklin Covey.*

She lives in Hamilton County, Indiana with her two children Cameron (18) and Auburn (15) and can be found at concert venues around the country enjoying live music from all genres.

Heaven Scent
Annmarie B. Tait

M om has been gone more than a dozen years but in some ways to me it still feels as if she left me just yesterday. The ache in my heart has dulled, but nonetheless is ever present. I miss her most when I am ill or troubled. Who doesn't long for their mother in times of sickness or distress?

Throughout the first year that followed Mom's death I experienced both grief over losing her, and burnout in my career. Bordering on a breakdown I decided to step down from a management post and accept a secretarial position at the company where I already had nine years tenure.

Taking this step meant surrendering a significant amount of salary and several perks. With all of that at stake one of the things that bothered me most was— would people think I was crazy? Would they look down on me as if I was demoted?

Mom cheered me on all the way through my career

and once I made manager, no one was prouder than she was. Not even me. Now all of that was about to change. I wondered if she was aware of what was going on in my life. And if she knew, would she approve?

Getting through those last two weeks tying up loose ends before I started my new position was exhausting. Mostly because I stayed awake every night wondering if I'd made a mistake. Wondering if I'd be happy and satisfied without the responsibility of being in charge and managing a staff.

Maybe I should have just resigned. Maybe I should have just kept going in my old job. The "maybe" factor robbed me of both sleep and sanity. Oh, how I ached to talk with her. Mom always knew the perfect words to soothe my frazzled nerves. Those days were gone and sorely missed.

At last came the day when I closed my office door one final time and left the building knowing that I'd return on Monday as secretary to the vice president, and in charge of no one but me.

As I muddled through the weekend I continued to fret over how things would turn out. By Sunday night I collapsed into bed bushed from worrying. Great, I thought. I'd be starting my new job with bags under my eyes the size of poker chips. I lay my head on the pillow and pictured Mom telling me to take a deep breath and ask God to guide me, and then I drifted off to sleep.

A few hours later I woke up to the aroma of a very familiar scent in the room, though at first I couldn't place it. I breathed in deeply and realized it was "Colleen" my mother's favorite perfume, which she used to purchase at the local Irish shop. As it wafted through the air I remembered picking up the bottle from her bureau and spritzing it on while sorting through her things one day. Then I inhaled even deeper comforted by the little mist of all that was left of her, the delicate scent of "Colleen". And now in the deep dark stillness of the night the scent of my mother lilted through the air and wrapped around me as soft and cozy as her favorite angora shawl.

In that moment my worries ceased. I knew for certain that Mom was with me, and even better that she approved. Whatever the consequences of my decision to make such a radical change in my life, I'd summoned the courage to sally forth with my head held high. As I laid my head back on the pillow the scent of "Colleen" slowly departed leaving in its wake a calm and enduring well of confidence in my heart.

The next morning I started my new job undaunted by the water cooler whispers of "career suicide" I heard when nobody thought I was paying attention. I took that giant leap forward and I've never looked back. I work hard, am well paid, and enjoy every minute of what I do. At the end of the day I go home feeling appreciated and wake up every morning wanting to get started with the new day. If there's a way to improve my situation, I'm at a loss to know what it is.

I am not favored frequently with the delicate bouquet of "Colleen". Since Mom departed I've encountered it only a half dozen times or so. Over the years I've noticed that Mom chooses her moments with great care—just as she tended her family with great care.

Five years ago when my sister was diagnosed with breast cancer I awoke the night before her surgery and caught a whiff of "Colleen" passing through the room and with it once again went my fear. I knew it would be difficult, even miserable at times, for my sister. But after that night I had confidence that she would overcome this disease, and she did. Her passage from sickness back to good health was a journey peppered with debilitating side effects and emotional stress, but she navigated through every storm and came out on the other side a stronger person for having survived the challenge. Two more times throughout her treatment the scent of "Colleen" roused me from my sleep. Each time I grew in confidence that all would be well.

Mom had five children. Why she chose me for this very special gift I'll never know, but I'm awfully glad she did.

Mothers are awesome beings. We are tethered to our mothers by invisible bonds as strong as steel, and occasionally if we are so blessed, as soft and sweet as the gentle scent of "Colleen".

———◆———

Annmarie B. Tait resides in Conshohocken, Pennsylvania with her husband Joe Beck. Annmarie has in excess of sixty stories published in various anthologies including, Chicken Soup for the Soul, Patchwork Path, *the* HCI *"Ultimate" series and* Reminisce *magazine. In addition to writing Annmarie also enjoys singing and recording Irish and American folk music with her husband Joe. You may contact her at: irishbloom@aol.com.*

Her Love Shined Through

Michelle Grewe

I almost missed my grandmother's story because I simply didn't listen well enough when she was alive. I didn't ask questions. I didn't get to know her beyond the woman who bought me a chocolate bar every time she went to get more beer, or the woman who stood up for me when the whole family was against me. Not while she was alive anyway. The most important things I could possibly learn about my grandmother, I learned from her ghost.

Her death was just about as silent as her life.

Sometimes our efforts are about as productive as pouring sprinkles over a dirty dish of melted ice cream. Empty nest brought my grandmother to drinking, and years after she quit drinking, with fierce determination, she was diagnosed with liver problems. At one point, we lost her for a minute. Doctors revived her and treated what they could, but her time with us was going to be short.

My grandmother smiled the entire day on Christmas in 1998. Her body was full of fluids, but she never complained of any pain she must have been feeling. She still helped cook dinner and handed presents to everyone, and the only difference between her behavior that Christmas and any other Christmas was at a few points, she had to sit down for a long minute.

My mother gave her a sweater as a gift and suggested she try it on. My grandmother responded, "Why don't you try it on for me?" I think she knew who would be wearing that sweater.

The next day, my grandmother was admitted into the hospital. She must have been wanting to do that for some time and wanted to wait until after Christmas, as if she knew her time was coming and just wanted one more Christmas with her family.

I visited her in the hospital, alone in the room with her as family talked about adult things behind in the hallway. (Even at the age of twenty, I still wasn't considered an adult.) My grandmother told me, and I'll never forget this...

"Michelle, you have to tell them to let me go."

While sitting on her deathbed, she told me what really happened in her moment of death before the doctors revived her. She saw a mansion. A big, beautiful, white mansion with a huge garden and a trickling brook. Peace. She felt peace like she never felt before. She wanted to go back to it. She wanted us to let her go back to it.

A few days later, the town of Wheeling, West Virginia, turned white from an unpredicted snow storm exclusive only to this area. Enormous flakes dropped down one by one during her funeral. I can't tell you what that means on a spiritual level, but I can tell you that storm was related to my grandma's death in some abstract way.

Months passed, and cancer started claiming family members. My father passed away. My grandmother's sister, who used to come to her house weekly to help clean the things my grandmother couldn't, due to her knees, too passed away. My father's sister... all three within a month of each other.

Then my mom's sister, my Aunt Jo, was diagnosed with breast cancer. The way cancer stole people from our lives... at that point we were very discouraged.

At some time during all the hospital and doctor visits, my mother drove north to be with her sister. On the way there, she had one of those accidents where the police reported that they had no idea how my mother walked away, unharmed, from what should have been a deadly accident. On the driver's seat of her battered car sat a coin. It was the Serenity Prayer I bought my mother on a coin years before in hopes it would protect and inspire; a coin she had no idea she still possessed.

At the hospital, my aunt Jo received surgery to remove the tumors. When she lay in bed, asleep from the surgery, my mother and uncle decided to use that moment to grab something to eat. When they returned to the hospital, the nurse spoke to them, "It was so nice that your mother could come visit her."

My mom asked, "My mother?"

The nurse responded, "Yes. Your mother came to visit, and she sat next to Jo holding her hand the entire time you guys were gone. It was so sweet."

My mom questioned further. "What did she look like?"

The nurse described my grandmother, exactly. My

mom responded, "That was definitely my mother, but she passed away last Christmas."

The nurse excused herself from the conversation and wouldn't speak of it anymore.

Aunt Jo later told me she also felt someone hold her hand before the surgery when nobody was there. Her sixth sense told her that it was my grandmother, but she didn't dare speak of it in fear nobody would believe her. Well, they believe her now.

———◆———

Writer and artist, Michelle Grewe is an Air Force Veteran, mother, and a human jungle gym. Published in 7 Books, Michelle's art is featured in her adult coloring and activity journal designed for spirituality and mental health, From Dust to Essence. *Websites who have featured her work include The Good Men Project, Popsugar Moms, Mamalode, and Blunt Moms. She writes about spirituality from a tolerant Christian standpoint on michellegrewe.wordpress.com.*

Hibachi Angel
Gail Blase

Katey died of a heroin overdose on June 13th, 2012. She was twenty-five years old.

We'd planned a dinner out together, to celebrate how well she'd had been doing with her recovery. We were finally getting our old Katey back. We had no idea that she had relapsed. When I got to her house, there was no answer when I knocked. I used my key to enter, called her name and got no response. Then I found her lifeless in her bed; she had been dead for six to eight hours.

Needless to say, Katey's death was the beginning of the worst time in my life. The years after that were so hard. Holidays, birthdays, family gatherings, and weddings left a gaping hole in my heart. I kept thinking she should be here. Our lives were changed forever.

I went to various grief counseling groups, where many people talked about "signs" they had received from their loved ones who'd passed. I wanted so much to get a sign from Katey.

At last, about five months after her passing, I was preparing a Sunday school lesson about Joseph interpreting the Pharaoh's dreams. I fell asleep while reading, and that was the night I had my first "dream," which was more like a visitation. As the dream ended, Katey said to me,: "Look up. Look down. Look around. Look to God." I immediately woke up.

I think she was trying to tell me that she is still with us. She's everywhere we are. And then she proved it.

My sister, Dee, had a birthday and we celebrated it at Ooka, a Japanese restaurant in Doylestown, Pennsylvania. When the hibachi chef poured oil on the grill, the flames almost reached the ceiling. The grill got so hot that we were forced to move as far back as we could. Dee took pictures of the flames until they died down. When we looked at the photos later, there was a very clear image of an angel in the flames. She was there with us at the birthday party. Our angel, Katey, came to my birthday celebration last night! I know she did!

Gail Blase lives in Upper Bucks County, Pennsylvania. She is happily retired after teaching kindergarten for forty-one years. She enjoys reading and traveling She visits schools and community events with Katey's therapy pit bull, Duke. She's a proud grandmom. She is always on the lookout for more angel bumps.

Jake is My Angel

ROBIN ALLEN

As a writer, I spend most of my time making things up when I am putting words down. So, when the unexplainable jumped from the page into reality, it took me by surprise.

Less than two weeks after my oldest son turned three, there was a knock at the door. Two uniformed officials were there to inform me that my ex-husband, the father of my oldest son, had passed. After a tour in Afghanistan, Jake came home only to die during a training exercise on base. It was the first significant loss in my adult life.

At first, the shock of the sudden void in our life left me hollow. I could not think about his death without a painful ache in my chest, but I did not cry—not until after the funeral. I had already moved on from the relationship with Jake. I was married to my current husband, and could only imagine how he was dealing with my grief over another man. As it turned out, I was fortunate. Not only did I find the love of my life, but an understanding

JAKE IS MY ANGEL

husband and loving father.

I was sitting alone in bed, reading a book after putting my young children down for the night. We did not have money for proper curtains, so we had blankets tacked to the wall covering the windows. As I sat there, absorbed in my reading, the blanket behind my head suddenly loosened itself from the wall and fell on me. My first instinct was terror, but for some reason I spoke aloud to the room. I said, "Very funny, Jake. You scared me!" My body shook with the initial panic and then relieved laughter. I could have brushed it off as a fluke— a loosening of the tack on a heavy blanket finally letting go, but in my heart I knew it was him letting me know he was still around.

Since Jeremy was so young, when I talked about his father I rarely mentioned his name. I simply referred to him as Daddy Jake. He had my husband at home whom he also called Daddy, but we wanted him to know about Jake and honor his memory.

Jeremy was around the age when many children have imaginary friends. I never observed him interacting with this friend, but was vaguely aware he had one. One day he said something I could not fathom him knowing, so I asked him where he got the idea from. With all the innocence of a child, he looked at me and said, "Jake told me." I tried not to look taken aback when I asked him who Jake was, but was not shocked when Jeremy told me it was the name of his imaginary friend.

For a while, I let it go. Fictitious Jake had not shown up in weeks, but suddenly resurfaced around the anniversary of Daddy Jake's death. Out of curiosity, I started asking questions about his "phantasmal buddy". The most

87

pressing question was how his Jake appeared to him.

Jeremy shared his vision: a boy, about his age, with light dark skin and curly brown hair became his friend. It was an uncanny description of his father as a child. I would have dismissed the accuracy as mere recognition from old pictures, but at the time we did had not acquired any. It was the first time I truly felt the chills travelling down my spine. It certainly made an impression.

It was years before we heard from Jake again, long after the fictional counterpart had disappeared. The five of us had moved into our first house and Jeremy was quickly making friends and growing up way too fast. I cannot be certain, but I believe Jake's spirit moved with us.

One day I was standing alone in my bedroom, hanging clothes in my closet. There was a quick but forceful pinch on my butt cheek. I turned around swinging my arm, thinking my husband goosed me; there was no one there. I will admit I was disquieted. It is not everyday one gets goosed by an invisible presence. The only way I could describe it was saying we had a perverted ghost living in the house. Only later did it occur to me it was Jake, making himself known.

Since then we have not had any outward signs, but we know he is here. The ghosts I see now are reflections of the father in the face of the son. It is in the way Jeremy smiles, the smirk he gets when he knows he is right, in his ginormous feet and curly hair. Even if Jake never shows up again he will always be here, giving me angel bumps when I look at our son.

———— ◆ ————

*All names have been changed for privacy reasons, except the author's.

Robin Allen is a stay at home mom by day, caffeine-fueled writer by night. She writes short stories and poems, plus book reviews at The Fiction Lane *thefictionlane.wordpress.com*. When not reading or writing, Robin dabbles in book photography and has joined the #bookstagram community on Instagram under the name @robin.bookwonder.

Jacob's Message
Anne Bardsley

I've been a believer in Heaven, angels, and signs from the beyond for a long time. When I first opened Anne's House of Angels, the news began to spread about a new spiritual store in town. My goal was to teach people about the serenity and peace that angels can bring to our lives, just as they had done for me during difficult times in my life.

Over time, the gift shop became a refuge for people with broken hearts who needed to feel the presence of angels. Some were deep in grief; others just felt lost. A mother who lost her son to crib death stopped in frequently. A few people who struggled with mental health issues would stay for a cup of tea. Teens who were arguing with their parents often dropped in, and elderly ladies just out for lunch often dropped in as well.

It was a precious time for me.

During this time, one of my new customers, Mary, asked if I'd consider a joint venture. She owned a hair salon. She asked if I'd be interested in showcasing a few of my favorite things in her gift shop: The Worry Box, angel dolls, jewelry, books, and plaques. It was a leap of faith for me at the time, as it was an added expense. But I did it.

One morning we were all home in a blizzard. Stores were closed. There was a state of emergency and we had to stay off the roads. Mary called and said, "Sit down! You're not going to believe this! Last night I was closing the shop early in the storm when I noticed a woman looking in the window. It was a blizzard out there, and I told the woman the salon was closed. The woman said, 'I have no idea why I'm here. I don't need a haircut.' Then she started to cry."

Mary immediately invited her in. She brushed the snow off her coat and offered her a hot cup of coffee. "I've just buried my six-year-old son, and I am so lost," the woman sobbed. "I've been walking for an hour and I don't know what to do with myself without him. I don't know how I ended up here."

My friend took her by the hand and said, "I know why you were led here." She led the woman to the salon's gift shop. The woman was suddenly surrounded by angels. That was when she spotted the book *All God's Creatures Go to Heaven*, a story about how children who go to Heaven are given animals to watch over. The boy on the cover had long, blondish-brown bangs. He was snuggling a fluffy, white rabbit in his arms.

The woman held the book in her arms, pressing the boy's face to her heart. She sobbed harder as she fell into Mary's arms.

When she could finally speak, she said, "This is my

son's face."

The resemblance was amazing, in and of itself, but when the woman opened the book, she saw the little boy's name was Jacob—the same name she had given her own son.

I'd have to say that taking the leap of faith with Mary's store was not the best monetary investment I've ever made. My store was never about the money. It was always about bringing the awareness of healing of angels to people. I'd have to say this angel bump was priceless.

Well done, Jacob. I'm honored we could be part of your message to your mom.

Jimmy's Chirping
Anne Bardsley

I n our neighborhood, everyone called my dad, "The Mayor of Willow Avenue." People who were fortunate enough to meet my dad, Jimmy Lawless, liked him immediately. He had an engaging personality that put people at ease right away. He mowed the lawns of elderly neighbors, without a request. He'd stop and help people on the road. Once he brought home a soldier who got stranded on his way home to Oklahoma. Another time, he brought six nuns home while he repaired their car.

With four daughters, our house was filled with neighborhood kids. My dad invited them on trips to feed the ducks at Eastern Baptist. He'd take them out in our boat, "The Betty Anne" named after my mom and me. My mom used to kid that he was the Pied Piper.

Our neighbor, Bobby, was one of my dad's favorites. One year, he'd gotten a pellet gun for his tenth birthday and my dad asked, "Bobby, what are you going to do with that gun?"

Bobby responded, "Shoot birds."

My dad asked, "But what if after I die and I come back as a bird, you'd shoot me?"

Bobby was horrified at the thought. "No! I'd feed you! I'd never shoot you!"

That was the beginning of "my dad being a bird" joke.

My dad left for work on December 8, whistling. Later that day he had a massive heart attack at the printing plant where he'd worked for forty-five years. It was a devastating shock. He'd planned to retire at the end of the month. It was so hard to fathom that he was just riding his bike and dragging Christmas decorations out of the attic. Now, hours later, he was gone forever.

I remember shopping for the kids' Christmas gifts in a daze. I had a full shopping cart of toys when, "I'll Be Home for Christmas," came on the sound system. I left the full cart and ran out of the store. I bolted from the store, and bawled all the way home.

The first Mother's Day after my dad died, I bought my mom a double heart twig wreath filled with plants and hanging vines. It spanned two feet and it fit perfectly to the left of her front door. Her porch is always filled with company: neighbors, family, and friends arrived constantly. I tell you this because it would be a very strange place for a red breasted robin to build a nest in the wreath. But that's what happened. We could hear her chirping as she filled her nest. At night, it sounded like a soft lullaby.

My mom joked that it was Jimmy watching over her. Then the bird had four babies, just like their four daughters. The coming and going of family and friends never bothered the birds. Eventually, the babies learned to fly and the nest was empty. We all missed that bird. Once again, Mom joked that Dad was staying just long enough to make sure she'd be alright.

That fall I entered a contest with a story about my dad giving us a memorable Christmas. He was driving home late one Christmas Eve, in a blustery snowstorm. Something was in the road ahead of him. He thought it was an injured dog and stopped to help. To his surprise, it was an elf who had slipped off Blitzen, Santa's reindeer. He was injured and needed a cast on his leg. Thank goodness, our family doc could help him. Naturally, Dad brought him home.

The next morning, the kitchen was staged for an elf's visit. My sister's highchair held two phone books on the seat. There were cookie crumbs and a tiny cup of half-empty hot chocolate in it. We had an elf in our house, and not one of us would wake up to meet him. My sister and I were even kissed by an elf!! We had elf footprints all through our house. It had to be true!

April 12th was my dad's birthday, and I was very sad and missing him. He would have been sixty-four. As I walked to my mailbox, a bird flew from a tree in our yard and proceeded to peck at my hair. It put on a little aerobatic show, twirling in the air. When I opened the mailbox, there were the usual bills and a grocery sale flyer. I closed the door and the bird chirped and sat on the mailbox.

Maybe I'd missed something. I opened the mailbox and felt way back. Sure enough, there was an envelope from a local college where I'd submitted my story. I sat on the curb and ripped the envelope wide open. I was so excited to see a check for one hundred dollars!

Tears were falling when the bird arrived once more to perch on my mailbox. He cocked his head and chirped. "I can't believe I won!" I said out loud, wiping my tears away. The bird sang a few notes and flew back to the tree.

Anytime I had problems or concerns with our kids, I'd retreat to the front porch and rock in a wicker chair. My dad's sign arrived again as I was sitting in a rocking chair on my porch with a cup of tea, just crying and praying. I brewed a third cup of tea and returned to the rocking chair. That's when our kitten started to make a fuss, whining and crying, under my hanging basket full of purple and white petunias. I noticed a bird watching me from a nearby hedge.

I put the kitten inside and just observed. The bird flew into the nest and soft chirping noises followed. I stopped rocking and remained still. Little heads emerged as the baby birds attempted to climb out of the basket to fly. One by one, they dipped toward the ground, but quickly caught the breeze and flew towards the hedge.

I got the message. It's time for my teens to learn to be responsible for their decisions. Even birds encourage their babies to fly.

A few months later, I got a spiritual reading with a clairvoyant, Debra Taylor. I asked, "What's up with the bird?" I didn't give her any other explanation.

Debra smiled and said, "Just know that when you see the bird, your dad is standing right behind it sending you love."

I bought a new birdhouse that Father's Day. It was made of cedar with a shingled roof. The opening was a large oval, big enough to fit twigs and other things. It was decorated with a few hanging baskets, painted shutters, and a wreath over the entrance. I thought it was fitting. Next to the house, I placed a squirrel-proof bird feeder. I filled it with the premium seed; nothing but the best for my dad.

On my birthday, June 30th, a red breasted robin began arriving with twigs. She nested in my dad's birdhouse. Four babies arrived shortly after. I loved the soft chirping of their young voices. I hoped they'd never leave.

I felt so honored that he chose to visit me. I'm sure he knows I got his message. After all, I am a believer. You know what they say, "Birds of a feather flock together."

———— ◆ ————

P.S. As I proofed this story, I looked out the window and a bird was sitting on my palm tree staring in the window.

Johnny's Tap Tap Tap
Anne Bardsley

M y husband and I are blessed to have a nine-ty-two-year-old friend named Fran. She lives in a white cottage in a local beach town with her mini-poodle, Teddy. To look at her you'd think she was a very sweet and friendly older woman. I thought that myself, until we learned about her adventur-ous life. She's piloted small planes, was a "Rosie the Riveter" during the war years, became an RN at the young age of 58, served in the Peace Corps, was a ballroom dancer and that's just to name a few of her accomplishments.

But, the best part of Fran's life began at a New Year's Eve Party in 1944 when she met The Love of Her Life, the man she would marry. Fran was twenty years old when this strikingly handsome, thirty-year-old sergeant in the U.S. Army walked up to her, introduced himself and with a smile she would come to adore simply said, "Hello, I'm Johnny."

On this particular New Year's Eve Fran's parents were having a difficult time encouraging her to attend the party. She was exhausted and didn't want to go out, but went, rather than disappoint her mom. Once Johnny escorted Fran to her chair, the two of them remained seated together the entire evening. You see, Johnny was tone deaf and couldn't dance, but that didn't seem to bother Fran.

When it was time to go, Johnny asked if he could see her again. Needless to say, the answer was, "Yes". Actually, that "yes" was only the beginning of a love that would last the rest of her life. They were married a year later.

Like so many, they had their secret ways of expressing their love for one another. Johnny's was a code. He would gently tap Fran three times on the shoulder. So even in a crowded room, he could use this simple gesture to remind her of his love. He'd "tap, tap, tap" and she'd simply smile. Johnny was also known for having a special nickname or saying for everyone. In Fran's case, it was "Peace at any Price Porter".

After Johnny passed, Fran moved in with her sister, Eleanor. One New Year's Eve, while Fran was in the hospital, her nephew Dennis heard three knocks at the front door, but when he opened the door no one was there. He called his aunt and said, "I know I didn't have much to drink, but I swear someone knocked at the door". A few minutes later, three knocks sounded again. He opened the door quickly this time, preparing to catch the prankster, but once again, no one, and another call to Aunt Fran. Fran just laughed and assured him, "It was just your Uncle John letting me know that he didn't forget the anniversary of our first New Year's Eve party." She told Dennis, "Don't worry, he's just telling me he loves me and wants to be sure I'm alright."

However, this wasn't the only time Fran would hear from her Johnny. There were two others as she recalls. Once Fran saw Johnny sitting on her bed. He said, "Do you know that I didn't think I could ever make it without you?"

She responded with, "I didn't know if I could make it either."

Sometime later, Johnny made yet another appearance to Fran, again sitting on the edge of her bed. This time he said, "Do you remember you told me you'd love me forever"?

She said, "I do remember that and I meant it." With that Johnny nodded and smiled. Then he was gone. She has often thought, *Was this for real? Or was I dreaming?* Well, she believes that either way, it was, Johnny's way of letting her know how much he loved her and that he would be with her, always.

Fran forever smiles, even blushes, when she tells stories about Johnny. I could listen to her stories for hours. In fact, I have. Sometimes her eyes glaze over with tender memories. I'd like to imagine that Johnny is with her then, holding her, as she shares her memories. When she tilts her head, I imagine she's resting her head on his shoulder. Johnny would like that.

Some loves last forever, here and beyond. Tap... Tap... Tap!

———— ◆ ————

This story was a combined effort with me, Fran and her sister Eleanor.

Keeley's Purple Butterfly

Nancie Moore

My sixteen-year-old daughter had passed away in April. I often found myself choking up from the ache in my heart and crying in pain at the loss of my little girl. This would happen at odd times throughout the day and night, sometimes because of a song or a picture or even a TV show that would remind me of her.

Other times, in the car or at the supermarket or at work, it would happen just because.

It was a warm late June morning. I was sitting out back in my yard reading and enjoying the solitude when one of those "just because" moments came over me. I started to cry. Tears welled up in my eyes. I couldn't see the words anymore so I just hung my head and let it all out.

After a few minutes, I raised my right hand to wipe the tears away, still holding onto the book with my left. That's when I saw it. A small, purplish-blue butterfly. It was sitting on top of the book and as I watched in wonder, it walked down onto my finger, opening and closing its wings slowly. My sadness was lifted as I stared in amazement at one of nature's most fragile and beautiful creatures.

Then I understood. In a time of darkness and pain, my daughter had sent me a message of hope! She was letting me know that she was always with me and that even if I couldn't see her, I could find her in the small unexpected joys of the world. That little butterfly stayed on my finger for almost 30 minutes, until I finally said " Alright Keeley, I get it! You're fine and I'll be fine someday, too. You can go now." And with that, she flew away.

Now I know there could have been a natural reason for that butterfly to do what it did. Did it just come from its cocoon and needed a place to land while its wings were drying? Probably. But the fact that it came to me when I needed it the most was, I believe, my daughter's doing. And there were many more times like this. Times of deep sorrow and pain followed by moments of joy and lightness. That's when I would say "Thanks Keel, I needed that!"

───────•───────

Nancie Moore lives in Gilbertsville, Pennsylvania. She enjoys house sitting and animal sitting, including horses. She is a fun lady who enjoys St. John Island, drinking wine and laughing with good friends. She also spends time in her garden with a butterfly.

Keeping Me Safe

SHARON GEHMAN

It was very unusual that I would be driving the family car, while towing a trailer. In fact I think it was the only time I ever did, and it turned out to be memorable. My husband always did the driving, but he was very tired on the trip home. He and our two children were all asleep while I did the driving this day. We were on the highway and I suddenly felt as though I was going to lose control of the trailer. It was swerving behind the car and it was very unstable.

I was worried, frightened, and starting to panic. I was thinking that I couldn't control the car or the trailer, and that this wasn't going to be good. Suddenly, I noticed a white car passing us on my left, and at the same time a total feeling of calm came over me. I was so calm that it felt like a vacuum in the car, with total silence, an obvious lack of any highway noise or any sounds at all. When the white car pulled in front of me I could see that it had a Texas license plate containing the numbers 925. It all happened rather quickly but at that point the trailer felt stable and I realized what must be happening.

I felt it must be my dad looking out for us, the obvious sign being the license plate on the car that passed us. Dad had passed a few years earlier. Dad had been stationed on an Air Force base in Texas when my twin sister and I were born on 9/25.

When I quickly pulled the car into a rest stop, I parked and my husband woke up and got out of the car. Before I could even tell him what had happened he was behind the car and in a very shocked and excited voice exclaimed, "I don't know how this trailer didn't come off!"

I replied, "I know how, let me tell you!"

My father was an excellent singer. His beautiful voice was frequently compared to some recording artists of his time. He sang on stage and at many weddings. I had always looked forward to him singing "Daddy's Little Girl" for our father/daughter dance, but he passed before he could sing at my wedding. He had performed it for many brides and their fathers.

To honor my dad, I used to sing "Daddy's Little Girl" to my daughter, as a lullaby. It always helped her go to sleep. One night I was singing it to her, while in her room trying to get her settled. It always evoked such wonderful memories of my father, and made me emotional.

While I was singing, my daughter and I clearly heard the front door open and she sat right up and said "Daddy!" We didn't hear anything else, as we would when he would come home and approach her room. It seemed we were hearing things until suddenly the bedroom door swung open as though someone was entering the room. Again she excitedly said, "Daddy!" But her daddy hadn't come home yet. The bedroom door was obviously wide open, and we both thought someone had come into the room. I told her, "That wasn't your daddy, honey, it was mine." I finished singing to her with a wonderful sense of peace as she fell asleep.

I used to keep my CDs in a holder, over my visor. I kept a few of my dad's recordings up there too. After dad passed, this was a precious gift of his music. Driving my car one day, a CD fell out of the holder and bounced off my knee. I thought it was odd, since it had never happened before. Absentmindedly, I picked it up and put it in the CD player.

It was Father's Day and I was really struggling and missing him. My dad's voice filled the car. I burst into tears when the next song played, "Daddy's Little Girl".

I'll always be my daddy's little girl.

———— ◆ ————

Sharon Gehman is a retired small business owner. She lived near Philadelphia, Pennsylvania since childhood, and recently moved to California, when she and her husband retired. It was their desire to live in Southern California near their children, who also relocated there. Sharon enjoys reading, gardening, and sketching, when she is not spending time with her family.

Making Daddy Proud

MARSHA WISE

My father died when I was eight years old.

I was a late-life baby, and both of my siblings had married and left home before I was born. It was just me, my mom, and our poodle in the house. Although I knew what they meant, it took me years as an adult to apply the terms "single parent" and "only-child" while describing my upbringing, because somehow, I never related to them.

My father chose to leave us by taking his own life, Labor Day 1975. Having been so young, it wasn't hard for me to let go and make peace with his choice. While he was alive, he was rarely home. His job as an over-the-road truck driver took him away a few nights per week; and his favorite barstool at the local VFW kept him away the rest of the time.

It didn't take long to settle into life without my father, and as I grew older, I thought about him less and less. My days were filled with school, friends, books, and whichever boy I liked that week. It didn't bother me when I visited friends' homes with dads present. I understood that was their norm, not mine.

I did notice my father's absence during high school, when the posters for the annual Father/Daughter Dinner Dance went up. I wanted a reason to buy a new dress and dance. I didn't like having to miss out on all those dances.

After graduating college, I was reading our neighborhood weekly newspaper—*The Enterprise*— where my own graduation announcement and photo had been published the week before, and found a high school graduation notice from a girl who had recently lost her father. She had chosen to write the announcement in the form of an open letter to him; about how she wished he had seen her graduate, and how proud he would have been to see his little girl in cap and gown.

When I finished reading it, I casually turned to my mother and said, "I wonder what Daddy would have thought about my graduating from college." I had been the first in our family to do so.

My mother, always the cynic, suggested he would have questioned why I had wasted all that damned money on a piece of paper. We laughed.

That evening, when I turned on the light in my bedroom, I found a surprise waiting for me. Although it had been hanging from the bracket of my wall bookshelves, about five feet away, my mortarboard tassel was lying on the floor at the foot of my bed.

Mine was an interior room of a traditional Baltimore row house, so there was no window or breeze that could have carried the tassel to the floor. No one had been in my room since I had left it hours earlier; and the only way it could have traveled that far was if someone had placed it there purposefully.

I picked up the tassel, replaying the conversation my mother and I had had about my father's response to my college graduation, and smiled.

"Thanks, Daddy."

———◆———

Marsha Wise, a Baltimore native, spends her days in many-pulled-taffy directions. She's a mom to three teenage boys, wife, realtor, tour guide, writer, and blogger. You can follow her misadventures at Pulling-Taffy.com.

The Moon Plant

Sarah Harris

I t started, as do so many things of beauty, with a
seed.

cΩΩ

My grandmother—whose name was Peg, but whom
I called Mom Mom—was an avid gardener. It was the
1960s, and Peg, her husband Jim, and their three children
lived in northern New Jersey, where the soil was rich and
fertile. With the talents of her green thumb, Peg's garden
on Park Lane grew lush and gorgeous. Her friend from
down the street, Helen, was her botanical equal; along
with stories of marriage and motherhood, they shared
gardening tips and horticultural lessons learned in their
own backyards.

They also shared their actual gardens. When it was
time to divide the black-eyed Susans, Peg would pass the
superfluous roots to Helen. When the hydrangea would
sprout a volunteer, Helen would carefully deliver it to
Peg's yard. Over the years, as their gardens and their

children grew, their yards began to resemble one another, due to the constant sharing of plants.

By the early 1980s, Peg's children had grown and were having kids of their own. It was time for her to sell the house on Park Lane. No longer needing the convenience of a neighborhood filled with playmates for their children, Peg and her husband bought a house located on a little bit more land, with a dining room and basement large enough to accommodate their growing number of grandchildren. But leaving Park Lane was bittersweet, and as a parting gift, her neighbor Helen gave Peg the seed pods of her beloved Moon Plant. It had been the prize of Helen's garden, and Peg was looking forward to bringing a piece of Park Lane with her.

Peg and Jim were happy in their new home, which they lovingly named "Roseland." The Moon Plant was happy there, too. Never before had Peg seen a plant so full and green and lush (not even in Helen's yard, if she was being honest.) The Moon Plant, with its graceful, snowy-white, trumpet-like blooms—which only opened in darkness, lasting through to the next morning—was fit to grace the cover of a magazine. It quickly became Peg's favorite part of the garden.

I, on the other hand, preferred the more playful areas of my grandmother's yard: the bridge that crossed the creek on the far side of the property, the funny round little Buddha statue, and the moss garden around back, which we envisioned to be the land of the fairies. Mom Mom's garden truly had something for everyone.

Peg's youngest daughter, Sherry, is my mother. As my grandmother was establishing her garden at Roseland, my family was living several hours away in a Northern

Virginia suburb. Our house was a mid-century split-level with a spacious lawn—perfect for a young, growing family. Aside from a row of pine trees at the back of the property, the yard was a virtually empty canvas when we moved in. My mother was excited to start a garden of her own, and naturally, she looked to my grandmother for advice.

After discussing climate, light, and zone-hardiness, Peg offered up some seed pods from her Moon Plant. Knowing that the Moon Plant can be finicky, my mother Sherry was skeptical. "Just plant them in a few different places around your yard," Peg suggested. "See what comes up, and go from there." My mom planted the seeds in four or five spots around her yard, and crossed her fingers.

The next March, right on cue, one tiny Moon Plant shoot sprouted in one little corner of my mother's yard, on the side of the house beside the driveway. All of the other spots where my mom had planted the seeds remained bare. But that one plant? Oh, it was happy. It grew large and lush and gorgeous, earning admiration even from Peg, the Moon Plant Whisperer herself. My mother's confidence in gardening bloomed right along-side that beauty and, eventually, her garden began to surpass Mom Mom's in abundance and diversity of plant life.

Eventually, my grandfather passed away, and Mom Mom moved into a maintenance-free townhouse. She no longer needed the spacious yard or the expansive dining room table to accommodate her large family. In fact, she was rarely at home at all. She ended up fulfilling a dream that she had shared with her late husband—to buy a condo in Florida that overlooked the ocean. She spent most of her winters there, enjoying the warm weather, her new friends, and visits from family.

Between her life as a snowbird, and the holidays and summer vacations spent with her children and grandchildren, Peg had outgrown her need for a garden of her own. She instead found joy in her daughter Sherry's beautiful piece of this earth... in particular, the Moon Plant, which continued to flourish decades after it had been sown from a few hand-me-down seeds.

Three years ago, my husband and I moved with our three kids to a town several hours from my parents' home. With this move, we ended up realizing our dream of choosing a neighborhood where we could envision our little ones growing up as we got older. We were Home.

Naturally, I turned to my mom for advice as I began to plan my Forever Garden. She gave me a few recommendations: ornamental grasses are good space fillers; liriope is perfect for erosion control on slopes; perennials will provide color and reliability; and you can never go wrong with roses. She also gave me some seeds from the Moon Plant.

My little Moon Plant, now in its fourth-generation, took its time getting established. It sprouted beside my driveway, but remained small that first year, nowhere near the size or lushness of my mother's and grandmother's specimens. It still brought me happiness, though. Each time I backed my car out of the driveway, I'd catch a glimpse of it. The sight of its foliage would bring me right back to my childhood days in Mom Mom's garden—playing the Three Billy Goats crossing the bridge, or chasing fairies with my siblings and cousins.

One morning in May, I heard the news: at eighty-eight

years old, Mom Mom had died. She'd spent the last days of her life exactly where she'd wanted to be: in her condo by the ocean, overlooking the water that she and her late husband had so cherished. I remember my Moon Plant had seemed especially bright and hardy that morning, its delicate branches appearing stronger than I'd felt, its graceful blooms as elegant as Mom Mom herself.

Time marched on, as it does, despite the loss of my grandmother. I felt the temperatures start to dip, and I watched as my Moon Plant began to drop its leaves and wither. The kids went back to school, and our family settled into its routine of homework, after-school activities, and cozy weekends at home.

Months later, after a particularly long and frigid winter, the weather brightened, and I felt my mood and my spirit rise along with the spring temperatures. We spent the afternoons playing in the yard; my kids would swing on the swings, hit wiffle balls, and put on elaborate plays with the neighbor children, all while I walked through my garden, seeing what was beginning to bloom and hoping that my new little plants had been strong enough to survive the sub-zero winter. Most of them had, but not all of them. I was particularly disheartened to see that there were no shoots or signs of life where my Moon Plant had been. I made a mental note to ask my mother Sherry for some new seeds next fall, when the seed pods would be full and ready to burst.

During one of my near-daily phone calls with my mom, I mentioned my poor, failed Moon Plant, and asked her for some seeds.

"Wait, you don't have a Moon Plant, either?" she replied, incredulous. "*I* was going to ask *you* for some seeds. For the first time in thirty years, my Moon Plant didn't come back!"

There was a moment of sadness on both ends of the telephone line, as we realized that the Moon Plant legacy, which had started with the gift of friendship, had come to an end; forty years of garden beauty was over, along with Peg's life itself.

Suddenly, my mother began to laugh. "She took it with her!" she said. "She loved that damn plant so much, she took it with her!"

It was too good a story not to find the humor in it. Had Mom Mom been harboring jealousy over my mom's flourishing Moon Plant for the past three decades? Had she taken mine, small and spindly, out of spite? Before we knew it, we were both laughing so hard we couldn't talk. Tears streamed down our cheeks.

A couple of months later, as I was getting the kids buckled into their car seats to head to preschool, I glanced towards the space where my Moon Plant had bloomed the year before. The space, which had been bare just days earlier, suddenly had a six-inch-tall shoot, with instantly identifiable leaves. I picked up my cell phone and dialed my mom's number. Before I could share the good news, though, my mom cut in, "My Moon Plant is back!"

"Wait, seriously?" I countered. "I was calling you to tell you that my Moon Plant is back!"

There was the briefest moment of quiet on the phone before my mom said, "It's May 13th."

"The one-year anniversary of her death," I replied.

Neither of us said anything for a minute, until my mom let out a quiet chuckle, "I guess she gave them back to us! Thanks, Mom!"

My Moon Plant has continued to sprout, right on schedule, every March since then. By May 13, it is in full bloom, remaining so until the end of August. I'm not convinced that my Moon Plant will ever match my grandmother's in size or beauty, but when I see my little plant, trying mightily to grow, and blossoming despite my not-yet-green thumb, it reminds me of Mom Mom's strength, beauty, and elegance.

And I sure am glad she shared it with me.

———— ◆ ————

Sarah Harris, mother of three, finds her Zen in her garden and in quiet corners of coffee shops when she steals away to write. You can find more of her writing at Live, Laugh, and Learn *(live-laugh-and-learn.blogspot.com) or get a peek into her life on Instagram (@sarah.keenan.harris).*

Mourning Dove
Elaine Ambrose

66 "S ee! The winter is past; the rains are over and gone. Flowers appear on the earth; the season of singing has come, the song of doves is heard in our land." (Song of Songs 2:11-12).

The lane from the house to the school bus took me ten minutes to walk. That's all the time I needed to remove the protective shell and clamor onto the bus to loudly greet my school friends. No one suspected my unhappy life at home, and I didn't want them to know. It was a routine I perfected over several years.

As I walked the lane, I became aware of how the surrounding farms and fields permeated my senses. I smelled the fresh mowed hay, felt the morning breeze mess my perpetually frizzy hair, saw the thick bushes of raspberries along the fence, and tossed a few into my mouth because they tasted like the coming summer. But my favorite sense was the sound of the mourning doves.

The birds perched in the trees at the bottom of the lane,

and I could hear their melancholy coo as I approached. During my childhood, I learned to mimic their soulful call. It was six syllables, with an accent on the second syllable followed by a single note and then three identical notes. The second note was higher, and I had practiced playing the call on the piano at home, fumbling with the keys until I found the right song. I played it over and over.

The doves seemed to sense my moods. On particularly sad mornings after a fight with my father, they would erupt with a chorus of low coos, almost as if they wanted to wrap a blanket around me during my walk. On days without drama, they often limited their songs, and I missed them.

I grew up and went away to college to experience my first opportunity at freedom. It was exhilarating, and I excelled. I returned home on breaks and during the summer to work on the farm. The doves welcomed me with their familiar chorus, and I opened my window each morning to hear and reply to their call.

After I graduated from college, I moved away and became immersed in the responsibilities of jobs, marriage, children, and life. When I took my little family to visit my childhood home, I always listened for the doves. They were waiting for me, and they sang.

It was in June after the first cutting of hay and when the raspberries were plump for picking when my father died. I spoke at his funeral and mentioned the mourning doves. Over the next few days, I heard them call. The sound was more mournful, and I mourned for all that had been and would never be. One morning a dove landed near the window, lingering just long enough to look at me, and then it flew away. That was my first angel bump.

Over the years, the doves have appeared when I needed to hear their song. The soft coo provided a soothing rhythm that calmed my angst. I needed and appreciated the repeated six syllables of tonic that was stronger and more healing than any medicine.

After one emotional and painful time in my adult life, I took a walk in a nearby park. The doves did not disappoint. Their sounds were particularly strong, and I stood still, closed my eyes, and absorbed the comfort with my every breath.

After that experience, I researched some facts about doves. I learned that the symbolism of mourning doves gives us optimism with its spirituality. Beyond their sorrowful song is a message of life, hope, renewal, and peace. I also discovered that they are monogamous in nature. Mates typically stick together for the long run and become very devoted parents. This fact only compounded my gloom because I was going through a divorce.

That didn't deter me from reading more about the birds. I was fascinated at how they are symbols of sacred life. They were mentioned in the Old Testament:

"See! The winter is past; the rains are over and gone. Flowers appear on the earth; the season of singing has come, the song of doves is heard in our land." (Song of Songs 2:11-12).

Many important stories in the Christian faith incorporate the dove. The Holy Spirit, one of the elements of the Trinity, is depicted as a dove descending from heaven during the baptism of Jesus. The scriptures also describe a dove as a symbol of hope after Noah and his overloaded ark had been on the water for forty days and forty nights.

He released a dove and it returned with an olive leaf; proof of life, trees, and dry land. The dove was a sign of new beginnings and deliverance.

The dove also represents peace. Pablo Picasso, the famous Spanish artist, when commissioned to design the logo for the World Peace Congress in 1949, drew a dove entitled "Dove of Peace-Blue." It is because of their simple and maternal nature that doves have become a symbol of solidarity and goodwill among nations.

My mother was widowed for 26 years. She remained at the house at the end of the lane for 20 years. I finally convinced her to move closer to me and to leave the lonely farm. As we packed up a lifetime of accumulated possessions and prepared for the final departure, we stood outside one last time to listen to the doves. They responded with a melody that broke our hearts. But we knew it was time to go.

Mom passed away on a cool November morning after the harvest was over. She had slipped into dementia and couldn't remember my name. I held her hand as she was dying, and I longed to hear the doves. But the sterile environment was cold and quiet. The only sound was her raspy breathing and my mumbled prayers.

Her funeral was in her hometown in her church. Several years earlier, she had commissioned stained glass windows around the altar. The centerpiece of the exquisite and intricate work was a single dove surrounded by a burst of light and color. During her service, the sun broke through the clouds and shone through the dove onto her casket.

Now whenever I wonder about her, I hear the coo of the dove. And whenever I hear the sound, I think of her.

The mourning dove's melody is an angel bump from my mother. I believe that to be true.

————◆————

Elaine Ambrose is an author, syndicated blogger, and humorous speaker from Eagle, Idaho. Preview her books, blogs, and events at elaineambrose.com.

Music from Heaven
Mary Stein as told to Anne Bardsley

Mary first noticed Jay while attending *Il Magnifico*, in which he was singing onstage. She asked a friend to introduce them, and the rest is history.

Jay was a judge-appointed advocate for children. He was an honest man with a great smile and big heart; his passion was always the children in his district. He worked relentlessly to make sure they got the best possible care. After he passed, Mary came to hear many stories from people he'd helped pro bono, and yet, he'd never mentioned to her that he'd been an angel to so many families in need.

Jay's other passion was acting. During their marriage, Mary was privileged to see her husband perform in dozens of plays. As he rehearsed for *The Allergist's Wife*, he fell off the stage and broke his leg. It was a bad break and required surgery. While convalescing, Jay graduated to crutches, but soon learned that going up the stairs was much easier than coming down. One night, as he was descending the staircase, he fell and broke his wrist—a break that also required surgery.

Mary and Jay lived in a two-story house, and after the second surgery, the only way Jay could reach the second level was by scooching up two flights of stairs, step by step, on his butt. It was a big house, so once Jay reached the second landing, he still needed to navigate a twenty-five-foot hallway to reach the master bedroom.

Mary and Jay devised a plan whereby Jay would sit on a sheet and Mary would pull him down the hallway on that sheet, and while she pulled, he would sing her a song. His musical tastes were wide-ranging and eclectic, so Mary was serenaded with songs such as "On Moonlight Bay," Sophie Tucker's rendition of "Everybody Shimmies Now," Muddy Waters' "I'm Your Hoochie- Coochie Man", Cab Calloway's rendition of "I'm Crazy 'Bout My Baby," and the song that Mary and Jay claimed as their own, "As Time Goes By."

Jay had many talents in addition to acting and singing, chief among them demonstrating his love for Mary. Before his passing, Mary never once had to fill her car with gas, make a cup of coffee, or empty the dishwasher. Jay always spoiled her, and they were happily married for twenty-five years.

During that time, they enjoyed movies, museums, travel, and theater shows. Jay also continued to sing. He had a deep, soothing voice. When his grandson Arlo was born, he crooned "Goodnight, Sweetheart, Goodnight" to him, while Arlo stared quietly into his eyes, mesmerized. It was one of many sweet moments between Grandpa Jay and his newly-born grandson.

Music was such a huge part of Jay's life, it seemed only natural that he would show her a sign in songs, but I'll let Mary tell the story herself:

"I wanted to share what happened to me yesterday, on the second anniversary of Jay's death. I'd recently started listening to music downloaded from iTunes onto my laptop. Because I like Cat Stevens, Carly Simon, and Judy Collins, those artists were my first three selections. Even though I had downloaded the complete albums from all three artists, when I hit play,' only one song from each came up: 'Miles from Nowhere' by Cat Stevens, a song that Jay had requested be played at his funeral; a rendition of 'Amazing Grace' by Judy Collins, which is a song that I chose for Jay's service; and 'Danny Boy,' as sung by Carly Simon—one of my all-time favorites. Also, inexplicably, 'Heat Wave,' by Martha and the Vandellas, another song Jay had requested for his funeral. We never did figure out the significance of that one, except that Jay would have wanted to make everyone smile."

Bruce Wheaton, his best friend, who introduced Mary and Jay, wrote the following in Jay's obituary.

"Jay was a unique mix of charming formality—he was known to wear his suspenders and button-down oxford shirts with shorts and black shoes— and warm generosity. And when he would get together with friends and family, Stein was always a great offeror of toasts. The toasts combined that sense of formality and gave him a context for expressing his almost sentimental warmth. He could make people weep before dinner with his comments about family and friends and companionship."

———— • ————

Mary Stein lives in Iowa City, IA, where she shares her home with Murphy, a year-and-a half-old Cavachon. Mary retired recently from a 35-year career in the educational sector, but fills her time by volunteering, reading, playing Mah Jongg, and walking. She is the proud grandmother of three grandchildren: a three-year-old grandson, Arlo, his brother, River and a three-month old granddaughter, Rigby.

My Grandmom's Hugs

ALEXA MORAN

When I was little, I discovered I had two passions: soccer and music.

My grandmother, a well-known pioneer of women's soccer, loved my passion for both. She supported every decision I made, and even better, she gave the most incredible and calming hugs. A hug from her could fix anything.

Losing her was the hardest and most gut-wrenching experience of my life. She'd always been my biggest fan, and the only idol I ever needed. Six years later, my heart still aches that I can no longer ask her what to do.

And yet, I still feel her hugging me. Her tight, warm, and comforting hug is all I need.

When my soccer team won the indoor championship, I could feel her hugging me, telling me how proud she was. When my team lost in the finals, 0-1, the 1 being one of only three goals I'd let past my goal post over the entire season, I could feel her hugging me, telling me how proud she was.

When I was given a coveted spot in my university's choir, I could feel her hugging me, telling me how proud she was.

When I was finally cast in a college production of a musical, *Spring Awakening*, I could feel her hugging me, telling me how proud she was.

When an injury and incredible pressure made me lose the fire I once had for soccer, I wanted more than anything to ask my grandmother if she was okay with my decision to stop playing. So, I did. And I could feel her hugging me, telling me how proud she was.

I recently got a tattoo, of the last thing my grandmother said to me. "Saying I love you, is never enough". When the artist was finished, I almost couldn't look at it. The concept was so overwhelming—having her words marked on me forever—not knowing if she would approve, but hoping she did.

As soon as I looked in the mirror, I started to cry, because I could feel her arms hugging me, telling me how proud she is.

Whenever I have a difficult task to face, or a complicated question to answer, I feel her hugging me, telling me how proud she is that I'm doing the right thing. I might not able to hear her word or her voice that I desperately want to hear just one more time, but it's good enough for me.

I miss her more and more every day. I wish she could be at my college graduation and my wedding, but if I always have her hugs at my most important moments, I'll be the luckiest granddaughter in the world.

———◆———

Alexa Moran is a senior studying Early Childhood & Special Education. She attends Shippensburg University in South Central Pennsylvania, where she works as a Resident Assistant and Learning Support Aide for a local school district. She hopes to one day be a special educator, and knows her grandmother is right by her side every step of the way.

My Mother's Coat
Sharon Love Cook

L ike many young people growing up in the sixties, I rejected "organized religion." Eventually I
stopped attending church altogether, claiming I felt
like a hypocrite. I had to *do my own thing*, a common
refrain back then.

My mother, on the other hand, had an unshakeable
faith. "Life goes better when you go to church," she
repeated. Her Lutheran practice played an important
role in her life. Over the years, she tried to lure me back,
with no luck. I had moved to the city and my life was
full. I was meeting new people, seeing new sights and
participating in new activities. I rarely gave a thought to
attending church.

The years passed. My mother had a series of small
strokes, the last one proving fatal. It was the Christmas
season. I went home to help and comfort my dad. After
sorting through my mother's clothes, I decided to donate
them to her church's thrift shop. Among the sweaters

and nightgowns was her favorite tweed wool coat with a fur collar, her "Sunday coat."

The volunteers at the shop graciously expressed their sympathy. "We'll all miss Mary," they told me. I thanked them and headed out. In the church vestibule, I spotted a flyer about the upcoming midnight service on Christmas Eve. My mother had attended every year. I always had an excuse: It was too cold, too late. Nonetheless, for some reason I decided to attend.

Snow fell as I ascended the church steps. I thought of my mother walking up those steps and felt a deep sadness. Inside, tall candles flickered while wind rattled the window panes. The mournful notes of the organ, coupled with the lateness of the hour, did little to dispel my sense of melancholy. How ironic that I would be in this church on Christmas Eve. *If only my mother were with me,* I thought. *If only she could see me.*

People arrived and took their seats, the cold air clinging to them. As it neared midnight, an elderly lady settled into the pew directly in front of me. Something about her coat caught my eye. It was tweed, with a worn fur collar—just like the one I'd donated to the thrift shop. A few moments later the woman slipped the coat from her shoulders. I caught my breath. My mother always sewed strips of white elastic inside our collars to hang from hooks in the closet. The woman's coat had the telltale elastic strip.

At that moment, the rear doors of the church swung open. The choir entered singing "Joy to the World." I rose with the congregation and joined them, loudly singing: "Let heaven and nature sing!"

I think Mom sang too.

Sharon Love Cook is the author of Granite Cove Mysteries, and the just released novel, Phantom Baby, *by Martin Brown Publishers. she is the VP of Friends of Beverly Animals (FOBA) and a cartoonist. Like her protagonist, Rose McNichols, she also writes for newspapers and does stand up comedy at nursing homes. She does not recommend the later as a career move.*

My Mom's Doll
Beverly Plant

I grew up in Toledo, Ohio. I was the eldest of two girls. My father reminded me often that he wanted the first born to be a male. I don't remember much of my childhood because it wasn't happy. My parents did love me in their own way, but the depression had affected their childhoods.

My mom's mother died when she was nine months old. Her father died when she was only seven. She was separated from her brother and sister and they were passed from relative to relative to be raised. During the Depression, there were many mouths to feed and never enough money. It makes me sad that my mom never had a loving childhood.

My dad's father died when he was twelve. With a large family, everyone had to pitch in to make ends meet. My grandmother didn't have any skills, except as wife and mother. There was very little financial help from the other relatives, who were better off. I feel very sad that my father didn't have an ideal childhood either.

When they married, neither knew how to raise a child. They did the best they could, but they didn't have role models. The love and physical affection was missing.

As a little girl, I craved physical contact. I wanted to hear the words, "I love you." I wanted to be hugged and cuddled. I wanted attention. I never wanted for anything materially—always had good food, nice clothes, and nice housing, but never that emotional display of affection that every little girl needs.

I remember when my dad brought home a special gift for my mom. It was a Little Red Riding Hood doll. She cried when he placed it in her arms. She treasured that doll. She acted like a little girl who finally felt special. It was her favorite gift for years.

I always looked for signs that my parents loved me. On my wedding day I hoped for an emotional moment when my dad gave me away. I envisioned him lifting my veil and hugging me tight. His cheek would be damp with tears. Instead, I was told, "You are on your own now. You are not our responsibility anymore."

After my mother died in 1995, I was in my thirties. I had so many things I wish I'd said to my mom while she was alive. It was suggested that I write her a letter and read it at her grave. I really didn't want to do that, so I just started talking to her. I told her I regretted how I treated her and that I wished we had been closer. I knew that she was a good person and loved me. There was so much I wanted to say to her. I felt like I was babbling. These weren't formal conversations, just periodic ramblings in private. I felt a bit better after each chat.

In 2006, I suffered many mini strokes. It forced me

to look at my life. I realized that I had been self-centered and selfish. I regretted how I had treated my parents. My father was still alive and I was grateful that I could tell him I was sorry. I couldn't just say I was sorry; I had to admit that I was wrong. I wanted to know how to make our relationship better. My father wasn't comfortable talking about feelings. He just said, "I'm glad I got my daughter back."

After a few weeks, my father called and asked if he and my step-mother could come over to see me. I was very nervous. I hadn't seen or talked to my father since I tried to apologize to him. I said "Sure". I didn't know what to expect.

My stomach flip-flopped. I felt like I was going to explode inside. It was very awkward. There was a lot of small talk and tension all around.

Finally, my father said, "I've been going through your mother's things. She always wanted you to have this Red Riding Hood doll. I had it made especially for her. Do you remember how much she loved it?"

I didn't know how to act. I was speechless. I recognized it as my mom's treasured doll. As I reached out to hold the doll, memories came rushing back. I remembered my mom holding this doll close, just like I wanted her to hold me, then and now. Tears soaked my face as I gulped back my full emotions.

Red Riding Hood has blond braids, the sweetest, most innocent face one has ever seen. Her eyes are blue. She's wearing a large, red dress. When you turn her over, a Grandma appears, with salt and pepper hair, and a white cap and glasses. Her face is loving and warm. Her dress is a tiny blue print. Take Grandma's cap off, and you have the wolf. I don't look at the wolf very much, too many negative feelings.

But why did he give it to me now, after all these years? Did my mom really hear me talking to her? It was like she whispered in my dad's ear, "I want Beverly to have my doll now." She wanted me to have something to let me know she loves me from Heaven. She'd forgiven me. I *was* special to her.

After my dad left, I held the doll close to my heart. I sobbed as I held her doll tighter. This was the closest I'd felt to my mom in a long time. Every time I look at that doll, the tears fall. They're good tears.

My mom and I are getting closer every day.

———◆———

Beverly Plant lives in St Petersburg, Florida. She has a son and a daughter. She's also the Grandmom of five children whom she loves with all her heart. She is an active member of Toastmasters International.

My Son's Message
Carol Taylor

My son, Tony, and I have always had a special connection. When he was a young boy, he was fascinated by the street lights. We'd take rides at night to get ice cream cones so he could see them. I loved those simple times we had together. As he got older, we were on the same wave length. He would be calling me on the phone; just as I was dialing his number. Many times, he'd ask me a question about something I'd just been thinking about.

Tony was a very thoughtful son. On his last Christmas, knowing how much I love Christmas decorations, he bought me two huge Santas. I'm not sure if he knew it might be his last Christmas, but he knew they would make me smile.

We laughed together. We sang together and when he got cancer, we cried together. He moved into our house so we could care for him. He never complained throughout his treatments. His biggest concern was what would happen to me if the treatments didn't work. He didn't want me to feel that heartache.

Finally, all the treatments failed. He was getting so weak and tired, we rushed Tony to the hospital. I wasn't there when he passed. I'd gone home to sleep. I was confident that I would see and talk to him in the morning. My husband called me back to the hospital at four in the morning. When I got there, he was gone. It was Good Friday.

I went into his room. I was sobbing. My daughter and other family arrived. After calming myself, I touched his hand and I heard him say, "Mom, it's beautiful here!" I screamed that out to my family. This was just like Tony. My son was so close to me, he needed to comfort me in my grief. He knew I'd need a sign to get through his leaving us.

We are still grieving. We know he is in God's hands and in a beautiful place. A few weeks ago, I was thinking about Tony's sense of humor while I peeled potatoes for dinner. I was deep in thought about him and I said, "Tony, let me know you are here." At that moment, a potato jumped off the stove top and onto the floor. I was so surprised I ran into the living room to tell my husband. I had to share it. Tony's sense of humor is alive and well on the other side.

I know he is still very close. His signs make me so happy. I hope he knows how much I love and miss him. I am so blessed that God chose me to be his mom.

———— ◆ ————

Carol Taylor was a hair stylist for 40 years and still cuts the family's hair. She's been married for fifty-two years. She has two children and two beautiful grandchildren. Christmas is her hobby. It takes her two weeks to get her collection arranged every December. She treasures her last gift from Tony in her collection.

Nan Meets Arlo

Anne Bardsley

My daughter, Jamie, lives in Colorado. She called me to say, "Mom, Nan is in Colorado today." I laughed because my mom passed away sixteen years ago.

"No, really, Mom," Jamie insisted. "Arlo has been playing with a little white butterfly for half an hour."

Arlo is my two-and-a-half-year-old grandson. He has piercing blue eyes and a head of blond curls. He is a little guy with a huge personality. He likes to wear an Irish cap just like my dad used to wear. Other days, he wears a cowboy hat. He also never leaves the house without his sunglasses.

His imagination runs wild. Some days he is Bob the Builder, a fisherman, and a jet pilot all within an hour. Within the next hour, he is performing "surgry" to remove germs. When his patients ask if they need to worry, he tells them "Yes, you should be very worried, but I will fix you." As he says those words, he pats his patient's arm for comfort.

Jamie was excited, as she continued her story. "They're playing tag. At first, he was chasing the butterfly, and it went behind the tree like it was hiding. Then, when Arlo ran around the tree in the opposite direction, it flew out chasing him. It's been the funniest thing to watch, and it's still going on! Arlo's doubled over with laughter. The butterfly soars high, then low, then even between his legs, but he can never quite catch it. I think Nan is loving this too."

I could hear him cackling in the background. He has a contagious laugh. My daughter and I both giggled.

"I called him over to sit for a minute and calm down," my daughter continued. "His cheeks were rosy from all the running. I asked, 'Do you like the butterfly?' and he looked at me, wrinkled his face, and said, 'Not a buffer fly.'"

"Of course, it's a butterfly," I told him.

"He put his hands on his hips, shook his head, and loudly said, 'It's not a buffer fly! It's Nan.'" It was the first time he'd ever said her name.

There is a belief that children are more aware of the spiritual world because they are so open and pure. As they grow older, they can lose that connection in our busy world. I am happy to report that Arlo is still open and pure to the spirit world.

The funny thing was that Arlo had obviously never met his great-grandmother, Nan, or at least I thought he hadn't, until that day.

—————◆—————

Jamie Bardsley lives in Colorado. She has a Master's degree in ceramics. She spends her days creating art in her home studio, chasing Arlo and preparing for her second child. You can see her work at jamiebardsley.com.

No Damn Funeral

CHRISTINE WILCOX

It baffles me to think that I remember. Exactly twenty- six years ago today, I was wearing a green and black sweater with cropped jeans and a tan leather jacket. About now, I was sitting in the stands at Ravsten Stadium with my friends while the sophomore boys football team played. My sister was at a dinner with the varsity volleyball team. My mom was at the hospital with her dad.

I don't remember what my sister was wearing— I think it was dress clothes, but I think she was also wearing her varsity jacket. All I remember is hearing her yell, "Chris! Chris!" and looking down at the stairs and seeing her looking up at me absolutely grief-stricken. I shot up, ran down a few steps and, remembering I hadn't said anything to my totally confused friends, turned and ran back up to say "My grandpa's dying," before I took off down the stairs again.

Kendra had already taken off, and she was faster than

me. I don't know what kicked in that I was able to catch up with her, but I did. I don't remember running that fast again since. But it really was like slow motion. And it really was like everything in every second was carving itself into my psyche.

We had all been waiting my entire life for this day— my life plus four years. Doctors had told Grandpa in 1967 that he had six months to live. He managed another eighteen years.

So my whole life and through the lives of everyone in my family, his death was an ever-present undercurrent in every conversation.

It's an interesting way to grow up. So many details of that night are still so clear to me. I still remember walking by the break room and seeing a haze of smoke lingering over the table, as all the nurses who were caring for my dying grandpa smoked. Ironic, like the emphysema that was claiming his life wouldn't touch theirs. My mom asked one of them how they could smoke and still take care of people who were dying from doing so. "You learn how to separate yourself from the patients," she said.

I can't separate myself from the way she said "the patients." I also can't forget walking into the room and seeing my mom sobbing as she held his hand. She was named for him and was his only biological child, although he accepted and adopted my grandma's two children as his own, just the same. Her name was going to be Radean or Ray Dean, regardless of what chromosomes she showed up with.

I remember with crystalline clarity the second I walked in there and knew that we had only moments left. I didn't know then how I knew— I just did. I bolted to the hallway and found my dad sitting on the floor. I said

"Daddy, Grandpa's dying," with tears streaming down my face, and he said "I know, sweetie," and he looked at me with a sadness I had never seen before.

I said, "No, he's dying NOW." He was gone not five minutes later.

Everyone was standing in a circle in the room. My Uncle Dale said a prayer, because he's the one who always gets nominated to say the prayer at family events. I couldn't breathe.

I took off down the hallway, my arms crossed in front of my chest, noting that it was nearly three in the morning and how ironic was it that Grandpa died around the same time that he would've normally turned off the TV and gone to bed anyway. My face was lined with tears that seemed to be never-ending. I passed a nurse who looked at me and detached herself when she realized she had nothing to offer.

And at that precise moment, when I would have looked to my grandpa for what to do next because my heart was broken in a million pieces, I felt him go into my soul, and I heard him say "Dammit, baby, stop it." It was so clear it made me stop in my tracks. I stopped crying. A sense of calm came over me and I looked around at my family and I knew then what I would come to understand more fully twenty years later— that life goes on, and love never ceases, even when our bodies finally fail us and we move on.

Grandpa—Bevily Ray Hudson (yes, his first name was really Bevily, everyone, according to the Warren County census)—was born on October 26, 1922, and died on October 25, 1985. And on October 28— the day we put him in the ground— he came back in a way that only he could have.

Grandpa had always said, "Put me in a pine box and put me in the damn ground. I don't want no damn funeral." Usually followed by something like "I'll come back and get you."

We would usually laugh it off and explain that the damn funeral was for us and not for him.

So while I'd like to think that it was all just a big joke to him and he just didn't want people crying over his casket, we never really took it as anything but idle words. Until Harley hit the house.

To give this some context, when my grandpa died, the nice men at the funeral home, with whom we had shared his good-natured threat to come back and make us regret any sort of ceremony, said things like, "We'll keep it small, don't worry," and "He's been out of circulation so long, I would bet it will just be family." Grandpa had been THAT sick for THAT long. I think the people at the funeral home knew my grandpa, but they didn't know the kind of loyalty a man like him engendered in his friends.

I first started to worry about the size of the funeral when we arrived at the funeral home. There were cars. LOTS of cars. There were people. LOTS of people. They were standing outside on the sidewalk, in the carport, everywhere. Walking in was like going to a rock concert—squeezing my way past people, so that we could get to the front of the chapel where the family was supposed to sit.

His funeral was so big, they had to open the overflow room and start piping the service through the speakers outside so those who couldn't get in could still hear. My mother shot a look to the director of the funeral home, who looked at us and shrugged, smiling as he cast his eye around the hundreds of elderly, potential client families who were in attendance. The funeral was beautiful. I didn't cry once.

When we got home, my mother and I went to Grandma's house across the street. She was perched in her recliner, cigarette smoke curling out from the ashtray beside her.

And when it was the most quiet and my mother and grandma had collected their tears, and we were just breathing—BOOM! The entire house shook. And then it was quiet. Eerily quiet.

I ran outside, and there was nothing in front of the house. I had half-expected to see a crashed plane in the middle of the road. And then I heard my mother.

"Harley, what the hell are you doing?"

I spun around— and I saw the car, which only moments ago was traveling eastbound down our street. It had somehow missed the house on the corner entirely, taking out only the heat pump on the side—and its passenger-side headlight had pierced the siding nearest the foundation directly under my grandparents' east bedroom window.

Harley's car hit the house, within hours of my Grandpa's warned-us-about-funeral. My grandma was inside, chewing on Valium like Tic-Tacs. My mom was outside dealing with her friend being taken away in a cop car. My dad was chewing the fat with the tow truck driver, and I was standing there at 14 wondering how incredibly powerful my grandpa must have been on the other side to have taken control of a motor vehicle— and crash it into his house. "I don't want no damn funeral" rang in my ears. I wasn't crying, I just wore a big smile.

———— ◆ ————

Christine Wilcox is a corporate communications executive who learned how to "write" stunningly dense, but informative articles at the tender age of six, when her teacher accepted straight-from-Colliers-Encyclopedia-copied text about skunks, mythology, and the solar system, as completely authentic work. She has worked in corporate training and communications for more than 20 years, and has a Bachelor of Arts in English Literature. A native Idahoan, Christine lives in Boise, Idaho with two spoiled golden retrievers who run her life. Her website is ChristineWilcox.com.

Our Christmas Tree Story
Patti Dille

This year was going to be different for us. Our tradition was to have my husband, Joe, take our two sons to a place where they could pick out a live tree and then cut it down. We had done this with the boys since my youngest, Matt, was able to walk. After our older son left for college, it was just Matt and Joe. Matt was the man with the saw. He would not only cut the tree down, but he would string the lights for us and decorate it as well.

Matt was 17 years old when he died. He was an accomplished Quarter Midget race car driver, and raced at many tracks in the northeast. He raced for 11 years. Matt was known for his sharp wit and his ability to make others laugh. Matt was a music lover, avid gamer, and someone who cared deeply for animals. He had a beautiful smile and is forever in our hearts.

We dreaded holidays, especially Christmas, without him. Just looking at the saw he used to cut down a tree, had us in tears. We knew Matt would want us to celebrate Christmas, so we decided to get an artificial tree that year.

We knew going on the Friday after Thanksgiving would be a good time to get a better deal. We had found one at Home Depot the prior week that we liked. When we went back, we found it had been marked down. We asked the guy in the store about the one we liked. But it was the only one left, the display model, and they had no box to pack it in. I asked, "Can you mark it down further?" The salesman went to get an assistant manager.

The assistant manager, Bob, came and said that it had already been marked down. I said, "Well, I have to tell you our story." I told him about losing our son, Matt. "We feel this is the tree. You see the sign on the tree? It says it's Matthews Fir Tree. We feel that this tree was meant for us."

The assistant manager, Bob, looked at us, rubbed his face and then handed me the sign. I asked again for a discount. Bob said, "I'm sorry. I can't give you a discount, but I can give you the tree at no charge." I gave Bob a big hug. Joe shook his hand. The staff got out their utility knives and cut the tree down from the platform, took it apart and the three of them helped us out to our car. We could not believe it. We were so touched by Bob's compassion and kind heart.

I wondered if Matt was whispering in his ear. I'm not sure, but I know an angel was with us that day.

———— ◆ ————

Patti Dille resides in Telford, Pennsylvania. She is co-leader of the S'myelin Faces MS support group. She runs a Stitch & Chat crochet & knit group. She is passionate about the Peyton Heart Project Kindness Mission. She also loves a good Chai Tea Latte.

Painted Ladies
TERRI ELDERS

At fifteen I'd not dealt with death before, so all I knew was that it meant goodbye.

That didn't strike me as fair. I didn't want to say goodbye to Grandma. Nonetheless, Mama insisted I attend the funeral with the rest of the family on that gray June morning.

"Dress in something dark; the plainer, the better," she said. There hadn't been much to choose from. I reluctantly donned a black straight skirt and slipped a black cardigan over a gray pullover.

Daddy wore his only suit, a midnight blue double-breasted outfit that he'd bought when he gave away my cousin, Neicie, at a wedding a few years back. It was a happy occasion then, but not today.

Mama had chosen a severe black rayon dress, but wore a string of pearls to add a little relief. My older sister, like me, had selected a skirt and sweater, but hers were charcoal gray. My little brother looked properly attired in a navy plaid flannel shirt and navy slacks.

I crowded with my siblings into the back seat of the old Ford. As we drove I wondered what she would look like. Mama had explained about open coffins and how we would all have a chance to see her before we went to the cemetery. I'd never seen a dead person, but Mama said there was nothing to be scared of. Grandma just would look as though she were asleep.

I couldn't picture her as anything but awake and full of life. Her eyes used to twinkle with happiness when I'd arrive on her doorstep, after I took the bus across town for a weekend visit. On Saturday we'd go to nearby MacArthur Park for a boat ride or to Bimini Baths for a swim. Every Sunday we'd head for a morning service at the Angelus Temple, and lunch afterwards at Clifton's Cafeteria. We'd both choose the salad sampler, four salad choices on one large plate. In the evenings we'd sit in her garden, nibbling kumquats and admiring the butterflies and hummingbirds that flitted around her Rose of Sharon and azalea shrubs.

Daddy pulled into the parking lot behind the church.

"Remember, kids. It's a funeral. No whispering and giggling."

My sister and I exchanged glances. We were way beyond such pre-adolescent behavior ourselves, and we'd had no desire for such childish interactions with our baby brother, who was only nine.

We filed into the church, with me trailing, and took our seats in the second row, right behind Grandpa Harris, the widower. I looked around. All my aunts, uncles, and cousins were there, equally somber in attire. So when the minister came up to the podium and said we were there to celebrate Grandma's life, I wondered why nobody was dressed for a celebration. Even in late spring, the room reflected the gloom of a frigid winter; everybody weighted down under black shawls and navy blue woolen cardigans. Grandma would have liked a celebration atmosphere much more.

Then Cousin Neicie swept down the aisle. Everybody swiveled their necks to watch her. Her platinum hair was twisted into an upsweep, and topped by a rose-trimmed cloche. Her fluffy pink, polka dot, chiffon dress swirled around her like a friendly cloud. She spotted my family, and slid into the pew next to me. I inhaled deeply. She smelled heavenly, like a flower garden on a hot summer day.

"Cheer up," she whispered, patting my hand. "Grandma wouldn't want people sad today. She's got her wish at last. I'm sure she's home with her Lord. We should be celebrating her life!"

I glanced to the right and noticed Mama and Daddy frowning in our direction. I remembered Daddy's warning.

"I'll talk to you after the service," I whispered back, then pursed my lips and tapped them with a forefinger. Neicie winked and fixed her attention on the pastor, who had approached a podium near the coffin.

He outlined Grandma's virtues, her devotion to her church, her leadership with the Women's Christian Temperance Union, and her years of teaching Sunday school. I'd never seen my father cry before, so was surprised when he pulled out a handkerchief and dabbed his eyes.

Then it came time for us to file up to the front, and pay our farewells. I overheard Daddy murmur something to Mama, as everybody rose. He'd been frowning. Neicie noticed my hesitation after I stood, and took my hand to guide me along. We stood together, gazing down at Grandma.

Mama was partly right. Grandma did look fast asleep. But her cheeks bore bright blobs of rouge, and her lips were painted crimson. She'd never worn makeup when she was awake, and I was pretty certain she didn't put it on to go to sleep. Neicie shook her head a little and then gave my shoulder a pat when she noticed my puzzlement.

At the cemetery the sun had finally emerged. I found it hard to hold back tears while the men lowered Grandma's casket into the grave. Then Neicie pointed out a beautiful tangerine and brown butterfly fluttering above the pallbearers' heads.

"I'm pretty sure that's a Painted Lady," she said. "Grandma loved butterflies. She gave me a book about them when I was about your age. I think that particular butterfly is a sign an angel has sent us that Grandma has arrived safely on the other side. That means that now she has her wings."

I nodded. That seemed to make so much sense to me, more than the concept of eternal sleep that Mama had tried to explain to us. Why would Grandma or anyone, for that matter, want to sleep forever?

Neicie always had a sweet way of looking at things. I finally worked up the courage to mention her outfit as we headed back towards the cars that would carry us to the reception.

"Neicie, I heard Daddy tell Mama that he thought it was disrespectful of you not to wear dark colors at a funeral. And that you have on too much perfume."

Neicie laughed. "I have so much respect for Grandma that I wore pink because it was her favorite color. I use *Quelques Fleurs* perfume because it's like a bouquet of all the different flowers that Grandma grew. When I go home this afternoon, I'm going to plant some pansies in my little patio, because those were her favorites. I'll bet they'll draw some butterflies and hummingbirds, just like we used to find in Grandma's garden."

I mentioned that I'd learned earlier in my French class that the name "pansy" comes from the word pensée, meaning, "thought."

Neicie hugged me. "So in the language of flowers, pansies mean 'thinking of you,'" she said, and I hugged her back, breathing in her delicious delicate scent.

Each time I've planted a garden in all the decades since, I've included a welcome mat of pansies and other plants that attract butterflies. Neicie convinced me that angels send us butterflies to remind us of the miracle that we're still loved by those who've had to leave us for another world.

I really miss Grandma and I love her Painted Lady visits to me.

———◆———

Terri Elders, a retired psychiatric social worker and a lifelong writer and editor, has been published in over a hundred anthologies, including multiple editions of the Chicken Soup for the Soul *and* Not Your Mother's Book *series. She co-edited* Not Your Mother's Book...On Travel.

Pennies Falling from Heaven
Lee Gaitan

Shortly after my father died, I began finding pennies on the ground everywhere I went. Of course, I'd found the random coin on the ground from time to time before—and once I even found a $20 bill in the parking lot of busy restaurant!—but this was decidedly different. It seemed every time I opened my car door and stepped out, there would be a penny right under my foot. I picked it up each time and remarked to myself how "funny" it was, but never mentioned my newfound ability to attract money—albeit in the smallest denomination possible—to anyone.

About a month later, a friend invited me to attend an angel conference with her. One of the speakers was a medium and he talked about communicating with those on "the other side." Near the end of his presentation, he selected a few people from the audience who wanted to contact loved ones who had passed on. I wasn't sure if this guy was truly gifted, but I thought it was worth a try. I raised my hand to volunteer and was more than a little disappointed when I wasn't chosen.

"Shoot," I whispered to my friend. "I really wanted to see if he could reach my dad. I want to know that he's okay."

My friend gave my hand a sympathetic squeeze and said, "Well, maybe he'll get a message from your dad anyway and call you out. I've seen that happen before."

At that I sort of drifted off, reflecting on the times my father and I had shared. A few minutes later, I came out of my reverie just in time to hear the medium remark very matter-of-factly that "found pennies" were messages, a kind of greeting, from loved ones on the other side. Apparently this was quite common knowledge in metaphysical circles, but it was a complete revelation to me. I snapped to attention and said to my friend, "Did you hear that, what he just said about pennies?"

"Yes, I thought everyone knew that. Hadn't you ever heard that before?"

No, I hadn't and it really stunned me. "Maybe I got a message from my dad today after all," I told my friend, smiling.

The next day, I was standing at the sink washing dishes and thinking about the "found penny" message. Unconsciously, I started singing aloud, "Every time it rains, it rains—beat—pennies from heaven..."

My voice caught in my throat and I felt an actual jolt go through me at the realization of what I was saying. I suddenly understood that I had indeed been finding pennies from heaven and not simply because of what the medium had said, but because of something else that for some reason hadn't dawned on me before. My dad, who possessed possibly the world's worst voice, had two favorite songs that he would sing over and over. One was "As Time Goes By." And the other one? Yes, "Pennies from Heaven."

I couldn't believe I had missed such an obvious connection every time I bent to pick up a penny. But I got the message loud and clear that day—and I didn't need even need a medium to do it.

———◆———

Lee Gaitan has worn many hats in her 25 years in communications, from public relations writer and television host to stand-up comedienne and educator. She has written two books, Falling Flesh Just Ahead, *and the Amazon #1 bestseller* My Pineapples Went to Houston—Finding the Humor in My Dashed Hopes, Broken Dreams and Plans Gone Outrageously Awry. *She has also authored chapters in the bestselling books,* The Divinity of Dogs *and* Feisty After 45. *Her work has been featured on the* Huffington Post, Erma Bombeck Humor Writers' Workshop, The Good Men Project, Mothers Always Write, *and* Sixty and Me *among others. She lives in Atlanta with her husband and dog.*

Pennies from Heaven

MARCIA KESTER-DOYLE

She comes to me in dreams, her smile radiant as she urges her horse up the side of Lone Mountain to a field of Indian Paintbrush. The wind brushes her long hair across her face as she studies the azure sky and points to a red-tailed hawk drifting overhead.

This is the how I want to remember my older sister Cherie; a camera looped around her neck and a bird guide tucked in her back pocket.

I want to remember her laughter when we were kids sitting in the back of the family station wagon and making silly faces at one another.

I want to remember our phone conversations that went well into the night, long after my husband had turned out the lights. At times, I had to muffle my laughter so that I didn't wake the rest of my sleeping family.

I want to remember the warm cinnamon rolls she made on Sunday mornings that we shared over a cup of coffee in my backyard garden.

I want to remember her gentle hands gliding across crisp sheets of white paper as she sketched magnificent birds of prey, her fingers stained from the pencils she used for shadowing their wings.

I want to remember the summers we spent picking huckleberries in the mountains and the flowers we strung together to make daisy chains on a porch in Montana.

What I don't want to remember is the night I watched a broken soul give up on life too soon; the woman in a hospital room who lay pale and unmoving under sheets as white as the pages from her sketch pad.

My sister had an eating disorder. She was killing herself slowly, and no one in my family understood why it was happening, or how to help her. Cherie never had it easy; married and divorced twice, she was a single mother raising a rebellious teen and had to work long hours to make ends meet. By the time she reached the middle-age years, obesity had robbed her of living a normal life. Food replaced the love and fulfillment she sought, but never found. It was the crutch that filled her emptiness. Loneliness and disappointment fed into her depression, preventing her from seeking the professional help that she needed. Something had broken inside her, leaving her heart cracked in too many places for anyone to fix.

In the fall of 2009 at the age of 56, my sister succumbed to pneumonia after weeks of being sick. My family and I urged her to see a doctor when her symptoms became worse, but she was a stubborn woman, convinced that she could fight the illness with simple, over-the-counter medications.

Cherie's son finally convinced her to check into the hospital once she started coughing up blood, but her lungs were already severely infected and had so much fluid in them that it made breathing nearly impossible. There was little the doctors could do to save her—the pneumonia, coupled with her obesity, was more than her body could handle. Her heart had become enlarged—three times the normal size—and one by one, her organs started shutting down.

My sister died in the early morning hours as we stood praying by her bedside. It was still dark outside with only a few stars sparkling in the west like silver glitter scattered across a black velvet sky. The moon had slipped away, its shadow swallowed by a blanket of thick clouds.

After Cherie's death, I was consumed with guilt for not forcing her to see a doctor earlier, and angry that she chose to give up without a fight. She left behind a son, a granddaughter, and a family who cherished her. It hurt to think that our love wasn't strong enough to give her the strength she needed to rise above the unhappiness that plagued her.

I tried to ignore the terrible grief I felt, but there were subtle reminders of my sister everywhere. The red-tailed hawk that watched me each morning from the tall pine in my backyard; the smell of cinnamon in the kitchen; the cardboard boxes her son had given me that were filled with her cookbooks, the glass figurines she'd collected, and a few articles of clothing that still held her scent of sandalwood and vanilla. But the most painful reminder of her absence was the sadness I saw mirrored in her granddaughter's eyes.

The finality of Cherie's death didn't hit me until a few months later when I found her favorite purse inside one of the boxes her son had given to me. I pulled it out, touched the soft, dark leather and opened the flap. Inside was a small cache of memories: my sister's comb, a few barrettes, pens, and several sheets of tissues. She had terrible allergies and never left the house without plenty of tissues.

I held the comb in my hand and felt a tide of grief wash over me, the pain so acute that it brought me to my knees. The memories unleashed a flood of tears that cracked the dam I'd built around my heart. The walls came tumbling down, and nothing could stop the deep ache that left a hole inside me that no one else could fill.

For weeks, I walked around in state of numbness and disbelief. Even though other members of my family tried to comfort me, there was no solace in the fact that I would never see my sister again. I felt disconnected from everyone and wanted time alone to work through my grief.

And that's when the first penny appeared.

It was old, the date barely legible on the worn, copper surface. I thought it was odd that I woke one morning to a penny sitting on my nightstand---I never carried pennies, and neither did my husband. I had been crying heavily the night before while thinking of Cherie. I wanted to believe that she'd found the peace she was looking for, and every day I had prayed for a sign of reassurance from her.

Later that afternoon, I found more pennies in the house. They appeared in the middle of my living room floor, by the kitchen sink, across my desk, on top of the couch cushions and on the windowsill.

Pennies started cropping up everywhere, and I soon noticed a pattern in their frequency. Whenever something upset me, a penny would magically appear. The day my husband lost his job and I was fearful of our future, pennies appeared in abundance. The same thing happened when my mother became ill and I was consumed with worry. I found the pennies everywhere while she was in recovery.

I didn't understand the significance of the coins. They seemed to pop up out of nowhere whenever I became agitated or depressed, and I went so far as to scold my husband for dropping them around the house. He promised me that he had nothing to do with them and admitted he had been finding quite a few himself.

The mystery of the pennies continued for several months until I discovered an article online about people who found an abundance of coins after the loss of their loved ones. I learned that the phenomenon is a common one for grieving families, and that the coins are a sign from the spirit of the deceased offering guidance and reassurance. The coins also signify value, and are used by the spirit to convey the message that the person they're communicating with is highly valued and loved.

I was further intrigued by the symbolism behind pennies. The penny represents "one", as in having a oneness with the deceased, and a unity in the afterlife with the spirit.

The penny also signifies a need for staying positive in the face of adversity, and for abandoning fear and uncertainty. The coin is a reminder from the spirit that we are always connected to them, even after death, and that they are there to help and protect us.

Once the mystery of the pennies was solved, I found healing and comfort in my belief that it was Cherie's way of letting me know she was still with me. She was watching over me and loving me, just like she did when we were children.

My sister has been gone for seven years now, but the pennies continue to appear in unexpected places. I have hundreds of them saved in a special jar, the copper coins glowing when sunlight fills the glass. I know now that she is at peace, having finally found the love and fulfillment she was searching for.

In my dreams, she is young again and smiling as she stands by the foot of the Lone Mountain in a field dotted with the bright blooms of summer flowers. The red-tailed hawk circles above, a symbol of her spirit riding on the wings of our love to a place where her soul can finally be free.

———— ◆ ————

Marcia Kester-Doyle is the bestselling author of the humor book, Who Stole My Spandex? Life In The Hot Flash Lane *and the voice behind the popular midlife blog,* Menopausal Mother. *Her work has been featured on numerous sites, including* Cosmopolitan, Good Housekeeping, Woman's Day, Country Living, House Beautiful, *the* Huffington Post, *and* Scary Mommy, *among others. She lives in sunny south Florida, with her husband, four children, one feisty granddaughter and two chunky pugs. Marcia can usually be found with a fan in one hand to ward off hot flashes and a jar of Nutella in the other, in case of a chocolate emergency.*

Polka Pick-Me-Up

Elizabeth M. Wood

I remained mostly calm as I drove my mother to her first cancer treatment on a sweaty summer day in July. Only my fingers gave away my nervousness as I repeatedly scanned through radio stations, searching for a familiar tune— anything I could sing to—that had a positive message or happy lyrics.

I focused on getting her there in time, pushing out of my mind the self-imposed guilt I felt for holding onto a secret, the longest time I'd ever kept one from my mother: I was getting divorced, and less than a handful of people knew about it. I decided weeks before that my news could wait. My mother had just been diagnosed with cancer, and needed to focus on healing; I needed her to be okay during a time when many other things in my life were not. Instead of sharing my secret, I made small talk with her about the ice chips and lip balm suggested in the cancer treatment video we watched together when I was in town for her first oncologist appointment.

Giving up on the radio's scan button, I turned the volume down as we pulled into the parking lot of the cancer treatment center. Patients in various stages of treatment came and went. Some had hair and some did not. My hands began to tremble on the steering wheel, as I silently wondered what my mother would look like in a few weeks and a few months. Perhaps she was wondering the same thing, too.

"You can just drop me off here," she said quietly, pointing to the covered drop-off area.

"Are you sure?" I asked, not wanting to let her out of my sight.

"It's fine," she said, her voice cracking just a little. The anticipation reminded me of dropping my children off for their first days of preschool, except I was certain my mother wouldn't be leaving from her first treatment filled with glee, holding a crayon drawing and chatting about new friends.

As we entered the drop-off zone, the radio switched on its own from soft background music to static. It sometimes does that, since my preset buttons are programmed for out-of-town radio stations. The radio must've lost the station signal, again, I thought to myself. I decided to fix it later. As the car slowly came to a complete stop, I searched for an uplifting word or phrase and the courage to utter it without breaking out into tears.

Joyful accordion sounds came to my rescue; polka music blared through the car speakers. Dah, dah—dah! Shocked, my mother and I stared at the radio. Then, we looked at each other— our eyes wide in disbelief. "Millie!" she exclaimed, tearing up and smiling.

"Grandma," I whispered. Goosebumps and giggles

ensued. Millie, my father's mother, was an angel on Earth for decades before she died in 2001 due to cancer.

My small-but-mighty grandmother always had polka music playing on the radio console table in her living room. We sat outside the treatment center, suddenly not the least bit concerned about cancer treatment or hair loss or death. I absorbed each of those playful beats of music into my bones. It felt like confetti in my toes, a never-ending kind of confetti that doesn't fall on the floor and make a mess.

Millie exuded love and kindness. She brewed gallons of iced tea for the dozens of family members that filtered through her home on a weekly basis. She stirred dozens of scrambled eggs with her favorite wood spoon for her children and grandchildren— serving up not only eggs, but also crispy bacon and her own blend of self-deprecating humor. She and my grandfather took me in to live with them for six weeks while my mother had back surgery; I was four years old at the time. After that, my world so revolved around her that I sometimes referred to my grandparents as Grandma and Grandpa Millie.

We kept in touch with handwritten letters after I moved away for college. Her letters often included tales of late nights when she couldn't sleep, what the tomatoes in her garden were doing (or not doing), and what Grandpa's snoring sounded like. She died a few months before I graduated.

Here I was, a mother struggling to comfort my own mother in her time of need. Millie lifted our spirits in a way that only she could, and made us smile during a time when that seemed impossible. One of my favorite stories she told was about how hard it was for her to behave appropriately during very serious situations, like church services.

According to her story, her mother carried a wooden spoon in her purse. If someone sang a note off-key, or anything went slightly awry, little Millie found it unbearably funny. Laughing in church, however, meant she'd get her hands slapped with the spoon. But she could just – not – stop – laughing. Even as she told the story, she laughed uncontrollably. It seemed as if she were finally able to fully let it out without any fear of the wood spoon.

When that polka song finished playing, my mother got out and went inside. I found a parking spot, a smile still plastered on my face. Thankfully, I've experienced plenty of close calls and lucky breaks in my life. During those times, I've thought that surely a guardian angel, or two, or three, were responsible for helping me. Even though I couldn't see Millie with my eyes, I felt her presence in my heart that day.

Millie was with my mom and that was the best medicine of all.

———— ◆ ————

Elizabeth M. Wood is a writer who lives in central Ohio with her husband and children. Over the past 15 years, her work has appeared on blogs, websites, newspapers, and magazines around the country. Elizabeth writes about embracing life's imperfections on her blog at www.ElizabethMWood.com.

Pop Goes the Angel Bump

SHANNON MASTRONARDO

In our cozy Pennsylvania neighborhood, we had a tradition of tying Mylar balloons to our mailboxes to announce special occasions: births, christenings, first Holy Communions, confirmations, bar mitzvahs, bat mitzvahs, and holiday parties.

Our son Keith, and our neighbor's daughter Courtney, were born just a week apart. Courtney was a beautiful baby and the center of her parents' world. She was Daddy's girl from the moment she was born. He beamed with pride just thinking about her. Pink Mylar balloons flew from her parents' mailbox when she came into the world.

When our son Keith, was born, it was our turn to beam. He was also a beautiful baby, and he brought so much joy to us, as well as to his three older brothers. He was the baby of the family and they never let him forget that. Blue Mylar balloons flew from our mailbox when Keith came into the world.

Our families became inseparable and intertwined.

Keith and Courtney walked to school together, and entered the classroom hand-in-hand. When she was scared, he stayed with her and calmed her.

Life was so pure for them, until the shadow of death entered the neighborhood.

Courtney was only seven when my husband had to tell her the sad news, because her mom couldn't say the words. "Sweetie, he said softly, "God called your daddy back to His house today. He'll be with God from now on."

It was heartbreaking to watch the two of them hug and sob. Keith, his brothers, and I cried with them. Seven years old is too young to lose a daddy.

Years later, Courtney and her mother moved to Connecticut. She and Keith kept in touch—they wrote letters, talked on the phone, and nurtured their friendship. They graduated from college, followed their passions, and stayed connected through Facebook. Keith remained in Florida after college, and Courtney stayed in Connecticut.

On March 19, 2013, Courtney had to hear that yet another person she loved had been called back to Heaven. At age twenty-four, just five days shy of his twenty-fifth birthday, our son Keith was killed in a motorcycle accident. He'd been coming home from a golf course, where his dreams of becoming a club pro were just beginning to be cultivated.

On June 28, 2014, Courtney came back to Pennsylvania to visit relatives. She stopped at Giant Food Store, and purchased two Mylar balloons. She planned to place them at two very special grave sites just a few miles from her childhood home. She bought a round Mylar balloon for her daddy's grave. She bought a butterfly Mylar balloon for Keith's grave.

Courtney shared this text with me after her visit to Keith's gravesite: "As I went to place the balloon on Keith's grave, I accidentally popped it. It made a "pop" noise, and within a minute it was completely out of air. And yet, one minute after that—it was flying throughout the air for an entire half an hour. I watched it soar as if nothing had happened to it. So bizarre!"

Courtney ran to her car to grab her phone, so she could capture this bizarre event for me.

Mylar balloons are known to withstand heat, cold, rain, and storms. They are long-lasting. I like to think this was Keith's way of telling Courtney that he'd be with her throughout all the storms in her life, and that he'd never leave her side. The balloon she bought for him was like the ones that flew on our mailboxes when they were born to celebrate their arrivals. And now, once more, he flew a balloon for her to announce that he'd arrived in Heaven.

The organization Compassionate Friends—a bereavement organization for parents that have suffered the loss of a child—uses the butterfly as their symbol. A counselor told Courtney that the Holy Spirit, with the breath of His angels, had sent a sign of compassion to her to explain to her that Keith's friendship will continue to soar in the spiritual world, forever.

———————◆———————

Shannon Mastronardo is a self affirmed chatterbox. She makes friends wherever she goes with her stories about her spiritual beliefs. Her hope is to inspire spirituality that surrounds all of us. She holds the record for the longest fitting at a bridal store while she shared her stories with the seamstress. She calls herself an energizer bunny for spiritual storytelling.

Pop-Pop is Tapping

ALEXIS WHIte

My grandfather, Pop-Pop, passed away when I was sixteen years old. He was my only living grandfather, and my brother and I were his world. We spent just about every summer at his house, and he spoiled us completely rotten. Whether we were visiting the Catskill Mountains, attending basketball camp at church, touring Washington DC, or just sitting in the back yard working in the garden or greenhouse, we were happy.

He loved to sit outside and whistle to the birds. He swore to me and my brother that he could talk to both them *and* the chipmunks—and we absolutely believed he could, though my brother will never admit it now.

Pop-Pop was a stern, old-school Irishman, but he was still the kind of man that would give you the shirt off his back. When it came to children, he was the biggest, softest teddy bear, and he would do anything for any child—his own children, his grandchildren, and even the children at the Shriners Hospital. No one in our extended family will forget the day he passed.

Years later, when I was married with two beautiful boys—a two-year-old and an eleven-month-old—I was paying a visit to my mother when she commented nonchalantly

"I saw the Red Baron today."

"The Red Baron? Who's the Red Baron?" I asked curiously.

"It's your grandfather. Whenever I'm going through a particularly tough time, or if I need some answers, I talk to him. Then I see a bright red cardinal. I never see them except when I've been talking to him, or when I'm near your kids."

"Mom, I think you need help!" I laughed. "You may want to lay off the booze for a while."

About two weeks later, my mom was entertaining my older son at her house while I was putting the baby down for a nap at my own home. Everything was fine in my little world of motherhood—until about thirty minutes later, when baby Connor woke up screaming at the top of his lungs. I rushed to his crib, and when I lifted him up, his little body felt like it was on fire. He also had a strange rash on his entire body. I'm not a paranoid mom (well, maybe a little) but this just seemed so strange to me. Half an hour before, he had been perfectly fine! I called the pediatrician's office, and they asked me to bring him in immediately.

Frantic, I packed up Connor and put him in his car seat. I called my mother and began to tell her what was going on—then, just as I turned the corner, Connor threw up all over the back seat. I'm talking The Exorcist type of throw-up. I had no idea what to do. Still on the phone with my mother, I pulled into a nearby gas station, went around and checked on the baby, and tried to clean up what I could.

That's when I saw what no mother ever wants to see. My little eleven-month-old baby was having a seizure. He was turning bluer and bluer by the second. I didn't know what to do. Should I call 911 and wait for the ambulance? Or should I drive directly to the emergency room? Connor was already in the car seat; I felt that I could get to the hospital faster than anyone could get to me. My mother agreed.

I hung up with her, and drove like a bat out of hell towards the hospital. I watched Connor in the baby mirror, and held his hand. Eventually, he started to breathe again, and while I was relieved, I was not relieved enough to slow down. I pulled into the emergency room, and got him out of the car seat.

The seizure seemed to be over, but as I held my baby in my arms, I notice that while he was looking at me with his eyes, the rest of his body seemed lifeless. I learned later that he had absolutely no muscle control—common after a seizure. While sitting in the triage unit with the nurse, I tried to calm Connor, but I could see the fear in his eyes. I struggled to hide my own fear.

Then, all of a sudden, I heard a tapping sound. I glanced up and saw nothing. Again, I heard it: tap, tap, tap, tap. Now the nurse and I were both looking around. "Where on earth is that tapping coming from?" I asked. The noise grew louder, and we turned at the same time to see a bright red cardinal at the base of the window, tapping with his beak.

As soon as we looked at him, the tapping stopped. He sat there and looked right at me and Connor.

The nurse turned to me, a look of bewilderment on her face, and said, "You know, I've worked here for over a year, and have never seen a bird just tap on a window like that, let alone a cardinal. In fact, I've never even seen a cardinal."

Tears began pouring from my eyes, and I felt a wave of calmness come over me. I looked at Connor and said with certainty, "It's going to be okay, Monkey." Then I looked back at the window and said, "Hi, Pop-Pop." Then the cardinal flew away. Ever since that moment, I have been a believer in angels.

I would like to report that Connor is now almost seven years old, and after five more seizures, a few more hospital stays, and some heavy meds, he is doing just fine. He's smart as a whip, with an extremely high IQ, and a place in the gifted program at school. That kid is going to cure something someday—febrile seizures, hopefully.

I'm sure a cardinal will follow him, wherever he goes.

———— ◆ ————

Alexis White is a single mom of two boys who are her world. They have taught her how to love and want to kill someone at the same time. She is a sales professional of 14 years in a man's world and loves the wow factor when they realize she actually does know what she's talking about! She loves the beach, but hates the sand. She is obsessed with shoes that kill her feet and loves a good sale!

Shannon's Lights
Paul Hackney

The day I buried my oldest daughter, I was driving home from the cemetery when the lights came on inside my brand new Jeep. I couldn't turn them off until I jokingly said, "Shannon, please turn off these lights." They immediately went off, only to come back on a few minutes later. As I turned down my road, several streetlights went dim. When I pulled up to my house, the lights in the Jeep went off.

From that day on, lights (mostly street lamps, but also house lights) continued to mysteriously turn off and on in my presence. Once I jokingly pointed to a light in a restaurant parking lot and said, "Shannon, turn that light out," and it immediately went out. Another time, I was getting out of a car with friends by a local market while telling them about the lights, and when I pointed at the streetlights and asked Shannon to turn them on, five of them lit up.

The three of us stood there in shock.

This happened for about five years, and then the frequency slowed down. In 2012, I was coming home from my now-wife's house when seven streetlights went out in a row. My daughter Heather was in active labor when it happened, and I immediately knew it was a sign from Shannon. I called my son-in-law, told him what had just happened, and that I was sure "Heather's having a girl."

"Unbelievable," he whispered back. "She just did." I got goose bumps. Now I realize they were angel bumps.

Heather named their baby Shannon. This little girl just lights up our world.

———◆———

Paul Hackney lives in New Jersey. He is an avid Eagles fan and has a passion for football. He coached high school football for many years. He is a writer, a devoted husband, and a fun Grandpop. He is an Irishman who celebrates St Patty's Day in style!

Sheila's Warning
Gwen Sanderlin

I met Sheila the first day of my new job. She was my peer as well as my team leader, responsible for training me. She was a tall, robust, pregnant woman, with red hair.

She was carrying a little girl who would also have red hair, and look just like her mom.

She looked very stern which intimidated me tremendously, initially. Once I got to know her, I realized she had the heart and soul of a very compassionate person. She was also a jokester and loved to laugh. Her stern exterior hid her true self well.

After I was trained, we became more like friends. She told me, "You dress too well to come to work."

"That might be been true, but I love to shop," I retorted. We both laughed. She mentioned her feelings on women being judged in the corporate world for their size. We decided to both get healthy and take better care of ourselves. The stress of a high-strung position took its toll on both of us.

I am a six-year cancer survivor. When I told Sheila my story, she said, "You've been through so much," and she cried.

As our relationship grew, we talked about ideas to escalate our careers. We tried to spark and ignite each other to reach that glass ceiling. At that time, Sheila started getting sick. She went from doctor to doctor until finally she was diagnosed with a rare liver disease. She was eventually placed on a transplant list when she was admitted to the hospital.

When I walked in to visit her in ICU, she tilted her head and said, "Gwen, you came!"

I played my sassy self, just like at work, and told her, "You need to get out of this bed and back to work girl. Come on... get up now. I'll even do that Miley Cyrus dance for you. You know I can twerk!"

"No way!" She laughed. "You have to do it now."

And I did. I twerked and shook and wiggled. This was for my Sheila.

Sheila roared with laughter. Her husband asked, "Where have you been? She hasn't laughed or even smiled since she was admitted."

I told him, "I am getting a butt paddle with her name on it. We will get her out of bed." We all laughed more.

"You can't stay here. We had plans to retire together," I reminded her.

"You'd wait for me to do that?" She grinned as she placed her hand on her heart. She reached up and tried to pull on the overhead bar as if she was exercising. Her husband asked again, "Where have you been? This is a miracle!"

That was Tuesday. When I left, I realized I hadn't prayed with her. I made a mental note to do that when I went back on Thursday. Her parents were called in on Thursday and I didn't want to disturb their time. Then we got the word that final arrangements were being made. I never got to pray with her. I carry that guilt today. I never prayed with her.

One week after Sheila's birthday, I stood at her service. They couldn't miss me. I was the only black woman there. Her mom came up to me and we hugged.

Back at work, I was a mess. There were constant reminders of Sheila everywhere. Another girl took her office. I couldn't have done that. I'd miss her even more.

I was working very late nights trying to break through that glass ceiling. By the time I left, the parking lot would be dark and almost empty. It was scary, walking alone at a late hour. I constantly looked over my shoulder and rushed to my car in fear of someone assaulting or robbing me.

One night I had a dream. I was in the parking lot when someone accosted me. I was kicking and screaming for help. Two people grabbed at me and tried to hurt me and steal my car. I was petrified. Still in my dream, I walked into work the following morning and told co-workers what happened. Sheila walked in just as I was telling my story and asked, "You're afraid, aren't you?" But I knew, even in my dream, that she was gone. She told me very softly, "Don't be afraid. *Do not stay* at work late anymore. Do not do it! Everything will be fine." She smiled at me as she turned and walked out of the room.

I woke up hearing myself screaming her name to come back. "Sheila...Sheila..."

That was her last visit to me. I don't work late anymore. I think of Sheila every day. I like to think she's my angel watching over me and protecting me from harm.

———— ◆ ————

Gwendolyn Sanderlin lives in St. Petersburg, Florida. She currently serves as the Project Manager and System Administrator for the NOAA Southeast Regional Office's EDMS (Electronic Document Management System). She's a long-standing member of Blacks in Government and Toastmaster's International. She is also a new Grandmom.

Sing it, Pop

Anne Bardsley

My father-in-law, Pop was a religious, obedient, and gentle man. He was overshadowed by my mother-in-law. I'd known him for over thirty years, but I never realized how sweet he was. When my in-laws moved to be near us in Florida for health reasons, I got to know the real Pop.

He was an extremely patient man with bright, blue eyes and a smile that endeared him to people immediately. He had great manners and always said, 'Please and thank you.' His favorite beverage was a cup of hot tea, "Two sugars and an ice cube, please." He was also a peace-keeper while his wife was alive.

My mother-in-law passed away first. Pop was heart-broken, naturally. The women at his assisted living facility began to swarm. He faithfully told them, one by one, "We can be friends, but nothing more," as he removed each hand from his arm. He was eighty-two at the time.

We were invited to every social at the assisted living

facility. One evening Elvis was in the house! News spread like wildfire through the corridors. I had a special invitation to be Pop's date for the show. Elvis arrived stuffed into a white nylon jumpsuit, wearing a black wig and sweating profusely. The women went wild. When he sang *Love Me Tender*, they sang along. Some swayed in their wheelchairs. Some danced to *Burning Love*, shaking their hips and laughing.

Pop made sure Elvis kissed me on the cheek and hung a moist red-striped scarf around my neck. He smiled really big when that happened.

My husband and I were usually the youngest people at the social events. Scott would dance with some of the women and I'd get a gentleman to box step with me. Our friends were having dinner parties and dancing on the beach to live music. Looking back, our time was priceless.

Our Sundays began with ten o'clock mass. Donuts and coffee and tea at our house followed. Pop scoured the paper for coupons. "It's a good coupon day, Anne," he'd say handing me a pile of coupons. Then it was nap time in a recliner for him, with our dog Murphy on his lap.

It was urgent that he get back for dinner. He had to make sure there were no women at his table looking for love in all the wrong places.

Pop and Scott became best buddies. Pop called every morning at eight and asked, "What's on the agenda today, Scott?" Translation; any doctor or lunch appointments today?

Scott is notoriously late, unlike Pop. Scott would pull up to fetch him for an appointment and he'd be perched on a bench waiting, sitting in his wheelchair, oxygen attached, blue soft cooler in hand, sunglasses and hat in place. He also usually had a dessert from the previous night's dinner, saved for Scott. "What took you so long?" he asked daily.

Pop relied on Scott to speak to his doctors. Pop was once very depressed, after his wife passed away. He called Scott to come over and sit with him. Fortunately, his doctor's appointment was that day. When they arrived, the doctor asked, "How are you feeling?"

Pop put his head down and was silent. He looked up and asked "How are we today, Scott?" He had tears in his eyes.

Scott told the doctor, "We're in the midst of a pretty bad depression right now, Doctor."

Pop agreed. "Yes, we're in a pretty bad depression."

We made frequent trips to the VA Hospital for various health issues. He always carried that soft, blue cooler filled with small juice packs and crackers. It was a five-minute ride, but we could starve on the way!

On one of our adventures to the hospital, I was singing along to Kenny Chesney's, "No Shoes, No Shirt, No Problem". The radio was blaring and I was dancing as I drove. I told Pop he should learn the chorus and next time Scott was in the car, I'd put it on and he could belt it out. Scott would be shocked. We practiced and laughed at ourselves. One of us laughed so hard, he snorted.

Pop passed away at the VA Hospital, on the hospice floor. He went gently in his sleep. His faith was strong and he wasn't afraid to die. He went to mass daily, said the rosary and woke at four every morning to say his prayers. He was ready at the age of eighty-four.

We had a big hole in our lives when he left. Our car automatically turned into the assisted living every time we drove past it. "Let's have a cup of tea with Pop," I'd say.

We decided to volunteer on the hospice floor, in honor of Pop. We took the eight-week training course and felt honored to give back.

One Friday morning, I was driving over the bridge that led to the hospital and I was thinking of how many times we'd made that ride with Pop. I missed him. I missed the soft, blue cooler, the big wheelchair and even his oxygen tank. I missed his eight a.m. phone calls and how his eyes twinkled when he told his old army stories. Sometimes he'd get to chuckling so hard, he gave himself coughing fits. I even missed those. I just plain old missed him.

I was getting misty-eyed reminiscing when, "No Shoes, No Shirt, No Problem" came on the radio. I sang along and stretched my arm out to the shotgun seat for the chorus. "Sing it, Pop!"

Tears were dripping onto my blouse when I swore I heard him sing the chorus. I laughed and cried more and I think I heard him laugh along with me. Once again, one of us snorted.

That day I had a co-pilot and his name was Pop.

Spreading Sunshine
Carol McAdoo Rehme

Humor does not diminish the pain—
it makes the space around it get bigger.
– Allen Klein

I slid the argyle sock over Mary's delicate toes and worked it over her heel.

Her husband poked his head into the bedroom. "Thanks for doing that. I can finish dressing her just as soon as I put away breakfast."

Mary rolled her eyes. "That man! He simply can't keep his hands off me."

"With a looker like you, who can blame me?" He pursed his lips into a low wolf-whistle, winked, and tossed the kitchen towel over his shoulder.

I grinned into my lap as I knelt at Mary's feet and started on the other sock. That was simply another in an ever-growing list of things that I admired about my friend. Her sense of humor was unmatched. Her determination to always choose joy inspired me.

Rheumatoid arthritis had struck Mary nine years into her marriage. Over time, the dreadful disease ravaged her body until it determined her course. Now, she relied on others for nearly everything: dressing, bathing, and meals. Yet she maintained a positive outlook, full of love and laughter and life.

I'd once accused my quick-witted friend of having a prepared arsenal of droll one-liners. "What do you do, Mary, stay awake at night to think up these quirky quips?"

"You know," she admitted, "I'm awake anyway." She avoided talking about the pain that peppered her restless nights. "And I decided years ago that no one wanted to be around a person who complained all the time."

"Complain? You? Why I've never heard you complain at all!"

Mary looked out the window. "Let's hope you never do."

When it came to the complaint department, we both knew she qualified for more than her share. She'd had twenty-four surgeries in forty-five years of marriage. And the last hip replacement came at a high price; a permanently-oozing infection that added a new element to her daily routine.

Mary and I had met over two decades earlier, me a new mother, her with a brood of teenagers and a married daughter. We'd quickly found common ground—church, writing, hobbies—and forged an easy friendship. Already using crutches, Mary was headed on a path of total debilitation; even so, I watched as she opted to wring all the pleasure she could out of life—and she swept her friends along with her. Life, we all agreed, seemed brighter in the presence of Mary.

For me, personally, she filled whatever role was most pressing at the moment: friend, confidante, sister, or mother. She sanded my life's rough edges and I loved her for it and always, always her sunny outlook and offbeat humor.

No wonder I was deflated when she and her husband decided to move to another state, where their oldest daughter would oversee their health during their declining years.

"You will call, won't you?" Mary's frail hand found mine. "And come west to visit us? Utah or Bust!" Her smile was watery and weak.

I could only nod.

Thank goodness for phone calls. They were our lifelines as her health declined further. Even when her spine separated from her skull and her daughter had to hold the phone to Mary's ear.

"You'll be glad to know I've decided to face death with humor," she immediately quipped. "Then it's less of a grave matter."

I groaned into the phone. "And hello to you, too. How are you today?"

"I'm skinny, weak, as helpless as a baby—and not nearly as cute," Mary admitted.

"Are you looking for excuses?" I tossed back at her. I swear I could hear her grin.

"No." Her tone sobered. "But I am looking for wings."

"Wings?" I blinked in confusion, still waiting for a comic comeback.

"Wings," she half-whispered. After a short pause, her humor returned. "After all these years, I figure I've probably forgotten how to walk. And, anyway, I'd rather fly. So I'm thinking God better have a spare pair of wings waiting for me."

Mary died one week later.

When you lose someone you love with all your heart—even when you know it's time—it is still possible to feel selfish in your own need. Your private loss and penetrating pain run deep. The day passed in a fog as I tried to process life without Mary. Regret thickened my throat as I thought about that last phone call. Had I remembered to tell her I loved her? My thoughts spiraled. Why hadn't I made an effort to visit last month? Did she know how much she meant to me? Why hadn't I told her goodbye? Had I ever really thanked her for her counsel, her friendship, her grace, her example, or even her very presence? What would I do without her?

Exhausted with grief, I tumbled into bed. But even in the dark of night, I couldn't put my heart and mind at ease. I lay on my back, staring at the moon shadows on the ceiling. The tears dammed up in me wouldn't wait anymore.

"I miss you already," I whispered. "I love you so much."

And that's when I felt it: a wispy, fluttering as sheer as gossamer near my cheeks. It trickled across my forehead and into my hair.

Almost simultaneously, I felt a quiver. No, no. It was like a gentle tickle. I felt a ticklish ripple in my chest, near my heart. It was so light, airy, and ethereal. Like a silent, delicate giggle or like... like...

Wings!

I sat up abruptly and looked around. The room was brighter. I could feel the warmth of Mary's presence.

"Oh, Mary," I breathed. "You did it. You found your wings!"

Her silent jubilance was tangible, just as her cheerfulness had been during her life. And, at that very moment I knew—like Mary—I, too, could choose joy. That's what I would do with her—and without her. I would choose to live joyously.

An award-winning author, editor and writing coach, Carol McAdoo Rehme publishes widely in the inspirational market. Her books include Chicken Soup for the Empty Nester's Soul, Book of Christmas Virtues, *and* Finding the Pearl. *As coauthor of seven gift books, she finds seeds of inspiration in everyday moments.*

Still Lighting Up My World

MARGARET GRAYSON

My dad died in 1985 when I was twenty-three, just three months after I moved out of my parents' apartment. I moved ten minutes away so I'd be able to stop by often. I was their last girl to leave the nest. In those three months, the relationship between my father and me blossomed into the relationship I'd always longed for. He was always a balabusta, but after I moved out our appreciation and love for each other skyrocketed. It was wonderful.

He was famous in the family for being a "Rube Goldberg." My mom would call him that and for as long as I can remember, when anything needed to be fixed or even constructed. My dad would come up with the wildest solutions, which were laughable because they were so ugly, yet super functional.

He made my mom flower boxes out of wire hangers for the apartment. When his belt broke, he'd alternate between an electrical extension cord and a piece of rope.

When my sister busted out of her wedding gown on her big day, Dad got out the needle and thread, fixed the zipper, and stuffed her back into her dress saving the day. He could fix *anything*.

He was also funny, easy going, and a big mush. I got the dreaded call one morning from my mom that he'd collapsed twice but wouldn't let her call an ambulance. I ran to their apartment and found him in shock. I told him I was calling for help. The following week he was gone.

I was, and still am, heartbroken. I'd realized I had just lost the first man I'd ever loved. Crying over past boyfriends suddenly seemed ridiculous compared to this.

He died two weeks before Thanksgiving. I was living in a big house with a roommate and decided to make dinner for the Christmas/Hanukah holidays for my mom, and my future husband's family, but it was my first holiday dinner.

I asked my Mom to come to come over and oversee the large bird in my oven. At the time, she and I were alone in the house. I wanted her to see how beautifully my boyfriend had decorated the house with fresh, deliciously smelling garlands, a tree, and wreaths, filling the house with that wonderful smell. He had also strewn white Christmas lights throughout all the greenery and tied everything with red velvet bows. When the lights were on it was better than Rockefeller Center.

You can imagine my disappointment when I plugged in the lights for my mom and nothing happened. I checked the bulbs. I checked the outlet. Nothing worked. I unplugged the lights and went into the kitchen to continue cooking. Suddenly I remember saying to my mom,

"It's cold in here," as I could feel a November breeze...in my kitchen. What? I peeked out the kitchen doorway to see my front door wide open and realized the all the decorative lights were on!

At first, I thought *intruder*, and being a nice Brooklyn girl I grabbed my bat running for the staircase leading upstairs, but then I stopped cold. I put the bat down and felt a warmth spread throughout my soul and I smiled. I looked at the beautiful lights, which were now *plugged in* and could feel my father's presence. I smiled and I cried with my mom. We both knew he had come back to "light up my world" again and to let us know he was with us and watching over us. He'd done a "Rube Goldberg" with those lights for us.

I knew this like I knew my name; it was the greatest gift I could have received.

Only a few weeks earlier, my mom, who was now always alone in the apartment, found a perfectly folded cotton handkerchief of my father's just sitting in the middle of the hallway floor. In my heart, I know he left her that handkerchief to wipe away her tears. She kept that handkerchief in her pocket for seventeen years, until she suddenly passed. She died seventeen years and one day earlier than my father. Every November 4th and 5th I remember them with love and yearning, knowing that as financially poor as we were I couldn't have been more loved. I was so rich in that department.

A year after my mother's passing I needed to go to the unveiling, but I was alone, estranged from my surviving sister. I asked my dear childhood friend, Parri Shahmanesh Sontag, to take me. She knew my parents and my mom loved her as much as she loved my mom's fried chicken, so I knew I'd chosen the right person. She drove all the way from New Jersey to pick me up in Brooklyn, just to drive two more hours to Long Island, New York, where the cemetery is. I brought my mom's cassette player and blasted Andrea Bocelli, her favorite singer, throughout the quiet grounds. Parri held me as I cried and to this day I couldn't be more grateful for her.

That night, when Parri was home with her husband watching TV, a lamp that was off simply turned on for a few moments and then went off again. No power outage could explain what had just happened. She turned to her husband and said that she knew that was my mom, stopping by to thank her for looking after me in my sorrow and for being such a devoted friend.

When she told me, I cried. I knew it was true. When Parri and I reminisce about these occurrences we still get goose bumps... comforting goose bumps. Now I know they are really angel bumps. I will always consider Parri to be the sister I was supposed to have.

Before my mom passed she made me promise that if my relationship with my actual sister was still nowhere to be found, that I would move to wherever Parri was so I would never be alone. I love you Dad. I love you Mom. I love you Parri. I am surrounded with love.

———— ◆ ————

Margaret Elizabeth Grayson was born and raised in Brooklyn, New York. She graduated from Brooklyn College with a degree in the performing arts/acting. She moved to Poughkeepsie to be surrounded by nature and live a more peaceful lifestyle. She's passionate about nature, animals, tattoos, and dancing.

Sweet Dreams

Linda Roy

When I was seven years old, I walked hand-in-hand with my father through the funeral home where the body of my favorite grandmother, his mother, lay perfectly still, awaiting our last respects. It was the first time I had ever been to such a place or seen a dead body, let alone one that belonged to such a beloved family member. At such a tender age, I was horrified, confused, and a little bit frightened. But most of all, I remember sensing for the first time, with any sort of depth, that this could all be over for any one of us. The sudden and stark realization of life's impermanence washed over me, and I sobbed uncontrollably as any young child would at finding themselves in such bleak surroundings. Yet, despite his own grief at having lost his mother, my father took me by the hand and we walked.

I remember clear as day saying to him the type of thing only a young child would dare utter, it was so blunt, yet achingly innocent. I looked up at him and said "I'm glad you're not dead, Daddy."

He just smiled, squeezed my hand and said "Don't worry, Honey Bun, that's not going to happen."

But it did happen. One year later, as he played cards at the church with a group of friends on a seemingly typical weeknight, while I was fast asleep, the world changed drastically for my family and me when my father suffered a massive heart attack and died suddenly. I was eight years old.

We had gone out to dinner. I sat next to him and we talked about everything and nothing. Just another family dinner, nothing special. Then he drove us all home, dropped us off, and I got out of the car and ran to the house waving goodbye without turning to look at him. I didn't say goodbye and I didn't tell him I loved him, because why would I on a typical weeknight? That's not the type of thing eight-year-olds usually have the presence of mind to say.

Children don't think about the fragility of life. Even though Dad had previously had a heart attack deep in the forest of Yosemite and had to be airlifted to a hospital, cutting our summer vacation short , I didn't make the connection that this could be life or death. He was my daddy, and besides, he told me nothing would happen.

Back then in the 70s, children weren't allowed to visit patients in their hospital rooms unless the illness was serious and they were next of kin. I was granted permission, but didn't want to go, for fear that he would look strange hooked up to all those machines, lying helpless in his hospital bed. Not at all resembling the big, strong, animated daddy I knew, but replaced by a frail, unrecognizable ghost-like image of himself. But there was nothing to fear. Even in his condition, he was the same, going out of his way to reassure me.

He was released from the hospital, we all returned home, and everything was back to normal as far as I could see. But normal would only last a few short months.

When I awoke on the October morning after my father had gone to play cards, I was surrounded by my mother, brother, and sister, all of whom shared the same stunned expression. My mother delivered the news that my daddy was "in the heavens."

This time at the funeral home, as I viewed my father's lifeless body in the casket wearing his favorite blue suit, and blue and white paisley tie, I did not cry. Instead, surprisingly, I remained stoic from the shock and sheer disbelief of what was happening all around me. Surely this couldn't be real. Just a year ago, he assured me this wouldn't happen. I believed him as I always did. I was his Honey Bun and he was my daddy, my ally. On the day my parents adopted me, he was the first to reach out and hold me. In family pictures, I was either seated right next to him or on his lap. What was I going to do without him?

When you lose someone close to you at a young age, you gradually become accustomed to the new reality. The idea of having one parent becomes second nature. Not because you no longer care for or love the parent you lost, but because that short period of your life that they occupied becomes ever more distant and life as you now know it takes its place. For a while, whenever I needed to hear his voice, I'd get out the old reel to reel audio tapes he recorded thoughts, ideas, and conversations on. I'd pour over slides from old family pictures and vacations.

But little by little, the sound of his voice deteriorated in my subconscious, along with those old tapes, every day pushing the memory further and further away, clouding the clear picture I had of him. Each milestone came and went without him; high school graduation, my move to New York, and when I met the man I would marry, there was no one for him to traditionally ask for my hand in marriage. Who would walk me down the aisle? It would have to be my brother. This time I felt my father's absence more strongly than ever before at the prospect of experiencing a life-changing event without him.

Since my father's passing, I'd had occasional dreams about him. They were always pleasant and comforting, about something real or imagined; a memory or something I'd wished would happen. But on the night before my wedding, I had a dream about my dad that I am certain to this day was a direct message from him.

I dreamt I was sitting on a folding chair in the church basement, the same church my dad was playing cards in at the time of his death, and he was sitting across from me wearing the same blue suit and paisley tie, and he was smiling. He reached out, took my hand and told me how proud he was of me, that he had enjoyed watching me grow into the woman I had become, and how much he wished he could have been there for all the important occasions in my life, this one. He went on to tell me that I had chosen an excellent partner to spend the rest of my life with, and that he was sorry he wasn't there to meet him, but that he approved. He told me that he would be walking me down the aisle in spirit and that he was always with me, even if I couldn't see him. He promised to be there to share in my joys and sorrows, the births of my future children, and throughout my trials and tribulations.

All I had to do was close my eyes and think of him and he would be there. Then we talked about everything and nothing, just like we used to do. I told him how much I wished I'd turned to hug him on the night he drove away, how much I'd always regretted not saying "I love you" one last time. He said he'd always known how much I loved him and that he felt my hugs. There was no need to feel regret or sadness. He was okay and happy just to see us happy. Even in death, he was the same, going out of his way to reassure me.

And in the dream, his voice came back to me clear as day. His mannerisms, the way he carried himself, all the things that I thought were long forgotten, were as real as when I was an eight-year-old girl with my family, Dad at the wheel of an old Winnebago, traversing the winding roads up a mountain leading to the redwood forest where my family vacationed one last time. It wasn't sad and it wasn't startling. When I woke up, the dream stayed with me very vividly, as it does to this day. A certain happiness washed over me, a peaceful stillness and a feeling of reassurance.

That day, my wedding day, I knew he was with me, and I could hear his voice again, telling me all the things I'd longed to hear throughout my growing up years. I truly believe he spoke to me through that sweet dream. And as I walked down the aisle, it made me smile. I love you too, Dad.

———— ♦ ————

Linda Roy *is the writer behind the humor blog* Elleroy Was Here. *A 2014 BlogHer Voice of the Year for Humor, she's contrib-uted to the* Huffington Post, Scary Mommy, BLUNTMoms, In the Powder Room, Humor Outcasts, Erma Bombeck Writ-ers' Workshop, BlogHer, Mamapedia, BonBon Break, Ten to Twenty Parenting, Project Underblog, Midlife Boulevard, Better After 50, Aiming Low, *and more. Her essays have been published in several anthologies, including* I Still Just Want To Pee Alone, The Bigger Book of Parenting Tweets, Surviving Mental Illness Through Humor, Only Trollops Shave Above The Knee, Clash of the Couples, Motherhood May Cause Drowsiness, *and* The Stigma Fighters Anthology. *No wonder her kids are always out of clean underwear.*

The Bench

DOROTHY PERNIE

All my very best memories include my grand-father. He was my constant support in a very dysfunctional childhood. On my eighth birthday, he surprised me at school by bringing the most delight-ful, white, fit for a princess cupcakes; each piled high with fluffy swirled icing and topped with a cherry.

He let me buy blue eye shadow at the drugstore when I was eleven and then, upon interrogation, denied knowing what it was. When he ran for local office, I'd accompanied him door-to-door, "politicking." My grand-father even allowed me to bring home strays until we were knee deep in cats.

In 1992, we sold our house in the city and stayed with my grandparents until our new home was ready. As is often the case, construction delays turned the few weeks into months.

My grandfather, having health issues, could only walk short distances, but every time he heard the jingle of my car keys, he managed his way up the driveway and into my car. Together we navigated the roads he used as a young man employed by Rosenberger Dairies. As only a 1940s milkman could, he'd regale me with old stories and gossip about people who once lived in the houses we passed. Too proud to use a store scooter or wheelchair, he would wait in the car while I ran errands. Then we would head to one of his favorite luncheonettes before heading home for his afternoon snooze in the hammock.

Soon after we moved into our home his health deteriorated. Afraid to die, he struggled terribly at the end. I loved him so much it felt a part of me died with him, and it left me wracked with grief. Two days after his death, still distraught, while lying on my bed sobbing, I suddenly felt pressure on my side and hip as if someone was leaning on me. Instantaneously I had a vision, in glorious color, of my grandfather alongside my husband's grandfather.

They were standing behind a bench where our two other grandfathers were seated. They were smiling while my grandfather pointed to a lush green hill where my young son and daughter were running. I felt an immediate sense of peace and stopped crying.

At the time, I took this as a sign that they were all watching over my children, however the true meaning of this vision has changed for me many times over the years.

In 2007, we built a house at the bottom of an old sledding hill my grandmother often visited with her great-great grandchildren. One day during a party, a hush came over the crowd. I looked over at the serene expression on my grandmother's face, and followed her gaze to the lush green hill where my grandchildren were running. It was as if time stood still, and I was again overwhelmed by that familiar sense of peace; as my vision replayed before me.

I lost my son last August to heroin. His addiction spanned twelve years with a few stints in rehab. He got a bad batch in March 2014 in Philadelphia that flooded area hospitals with over sixty critically ill addicts. He was a John Doe at one of those hospitals for four days, and after awaking from a coma, he spent the next four months on dialysis. My mother took him in, she and my stepdad nursed him back to health, took him to his appointments, therapy, and meetings. She gave us all a chance to have our Brandon back for a short time, he was able to visit with his children two days before he died.

I was in the car on the way home that gray and rainy afternoon when Judy Garland singing "Somewhere Over the Rainbow" starting playing on the radio. I felt an immediate sense of doom and was overcome by sadness. Within the hour my mother called to tell me that he had overdosed and was taken to the hospital where he died shortly after.

I know now that the pain and anguish I felt in the car that day was his. The sadness I felt was his, unable to withstand the monster. He did not wish to die. As I write this, I truly believe, with every ounce of my being, that the grandfathers have scooched over to make room for him on that bench. He is finally home.

Dorothy Pernie lives at the foot of an old sledding hill, a magical place full of family, friends, fun, and shenanigans. On misty mornings, you can find her in the garden, sipping coffee, planning new adventures, or contemplating world peace.

The Quilt and the Angel Stitch

Nancy BISHOP Stott

Six years ago, I married my high school sweetheart Dave, after we had been "lost" to each other for well over forty years. After reconnecting through social media, we had become e-mail buddies, but nothing more, as we were both married with grown children and grandchildren. Our spouses knew we were in each other's lives once again, and often asked after us.

Unfortunately, Dave's wife, Kris, died very suddenly from a brain aneurysm, leaving a huge void in his life, the lives of their children, and Kris' community of quilters and needlework enthusiasts.

Dave and I continued our e-mail relationship in support of each other's mutual losses—I comforted him after the death of his wife, and he comforted me as my thirty-eight-year marriage came to an end. As time flew by, we realized we loved each other very much, and thanks to strong faith, pure love, the magic of technology, and many flights from Atlanta to Chicago and back, we married in 2010.

My mom had gone into hospice, and was always cold, so I decided to make her a warm lap quilt for quite possibly her last Christmas on Earth. I selected fabrics from the stash that Kris had left behind, and started to plan my work. Now, I am not a true quilter, but I gave this project my all. During the entire cutting, stitching, ironing, and creating process I felt a constant, calming presence, and a gentle breeze with a clove fragrance. Kris used to make potpourri from cloves, so I always think of her when the scent is in the air. It also seemed to me that the quilt's seams were being sewn magically because the edges were coming out perfectly square, and the finishing details were proving far too easy to for my ability alone.

I knew then that Kris was pleased that I had come back into Dave's life and was helping care for their family. In return, she'd decided to guide me through choosing her fabrics, using her iron, and holding the quilt straight as each stitch was machine-sewn.

Was it an angel bump? Was she comforted that her family was okay? Was it a sign that she was at peace with me loving her family, and making sure that she was always remembered in our busy lives? I can't be sure. But I do know that in my world it was much more than an angel bump. It was peace passing between two women who had never met, over a quilt designed to give warmth and love to someone who at age ninety-two had also loved her family very much.

The quilt was placed over my mom as she entered Heaven, and we believe to this day that she was met by Kris and the others who'd loved her here on Earth.

Nancy Bishop Stott is a sixty seven year old transplanted southern belle who married her high school sweetheart six years ago. Life took them in different directions for over forty three years before the reconnected through the internet angels. They realized they still loved each other and hope to live the rest of their fairy tale days happily ever after.

Three Plates

PHILIP SULLIVAN

The job market in New Hampshire where I lived was very weak at the time and I really needed a change. So I packed up all my belongings and moved to the state of Florida. At the time I only had two family members living in Florida, my paternal grandparents.

Nana and Papa were my closest living blood relatives. I tried to visit them at least once a month. It was a three-hour drive so I usually spent the weekend with them. My grandparents were a very close couple. Papa used to tell us how they met on Valentine's Day. It was love at first sight.

When I first arrived in Florida both Nana and Papa were in pretty good shape. They would throw dinner parties. They volunteered with their church. Papa worked for H&R Block and Nana would hold open houses for a local realtor to supplement their income. Our favorite activities together were golfing and watching Patriots, Red

Sox, Bruins, or Celtics games depending on the season. Papa and I would have a few beers while watching the games. Sometimes Nana would join us. On Sundays we would go to church.

As time went on Nana's memory started to fade. She had developed Alzheimer's disease. Papa did his best to keep Nana at home. He hired a string of home health aides to help them around the house. But as time went on Nana got more and more confused. This confusion led Nana to wander off from time to time. The local police started to become accustomed to picking her up and driving her home. She would have driven off, but Papa would always make sure she didn't have the car keys. They didn't have a silver alert system back then.

Eventually Nana's confusion led to violent episodes. Even though her mind was going she remained physically a strong woman. In her younger years she used to arm wrestle my father's college classmates and win. These violent outbreaks became more than Papa could handle. It broke his heart but he had to put her in a nursing home.

As far as nursing homes went this was one of the best ones I ever seen. It was clean and had a very nice common area for families to gather and spend time with their loved ones. It had an ice cream parlor and they even had church on Sundays.

Papa would visit her every day for most of the day. I would visit on weekends. We would take Nana for walks on the property. They used to sit on a bench under an oak tree that Papa would call an apple tree. He called it an apple tree because of the old song "Don't Sit Under the Apple Tree" (with Anyone Else but Me). Papa love loved Nana so much.

When Christmas time came Papa wanted to bring Nana home. We planned what might be our last Christmas together. I was a CNA at the time so I was more than able to take care of Nana over the holiday. That Christmas, my wife Amanda and I made the three-hour trip and the four of us spent a very nice Christmas together.

When spring arrived my brother came down for a visit. He spent most of the week with Nana and Papa. From what I'm told they had a very good time together. I picked my brother up on February 13 so we could take him to the airport the next day. Early Valentine's morning the phone rang, it was Papa. Nana had passed away on Valentine's Day; the anniversary of the day they met. Papa had lost the love of his life. He was heartbroken. My brother postponed his flight and we rushed to Papa's side. We helped him with the funeral arrangements and the rest of the family flew in for the funeral. We picked out a dress and an urn with praying hands on it.

Now that Nana had gone I still made the trip to visit Papa as much as I could. Papa was still in good shape. We would go golfing with his friends. I could out drive them but they almost always would win the hole.

On the first trip Amanda and I made to visit my grandfather we spent the day watching sports, drinking beer, and reminiscing about Nana. Papa had placed the praying hands urn in Nana's chair but moved it to the top of the television so I could sit with him. We were sitting in his living room and a bird flew up to the window and started tapping on it. I asked Papa about it and he said, "It's a common yellow throat that has been tapping on the window for a week or so."

I joked and said, "I think Nana sent him to watch over you."

For the next two or three years every day that bird would tap on the window. I said, "Nana must really want to keep an eye on you, Papa." He grinned but he wiped a tear from his eye. Then one visit the bird did not show up. Papa didn't know what happened to his friend. He or she just stopped coming.

My very next visit something peculiar happened. A cardinal started tapping on the window. This cardinal started coming every day for a few months and then stopped. Papa said, "Nana is still watching out for me."

After a few months, the cardinal stopped coming. Then, to our amazement, a little chickadee started tapping on the window. The chickadee was more ambitious than the other two. One day when we were grilling in the back yard one of us opened the back door and the chickadee flew in. It flew around the house landing from time to time. It took us about an hour to guide it back out safely. Nana must have wanted to take a closer look. The chickadee continued tapping on the window daily, but never tried to get back into the house again.

Papa's health was declining and he decided he could no longer live on his own. My brother had a big house up north with an extra room so they decided he should live there and sell the house. As the closest relatives the task of cleaning the house fell to Amanda and me. It was our task to sort through a lifetime of Nana and Papa's memories. So we rented a dumpster to get rid of what we couldn't salvage. We rented a U-Haul to bring the rest of their possessions up north for the family to decide what to do with, and cleaned every inch of the house.

Nana's nightstand hadn't been touched since she passed away. I was amazed to find what was in there. I pulled out three plates with pictures of birds on them. One plate had a common yellow throat on it. One plate had a cardinal on it. And one plate had a chickadee on it. These were the very same species of birds that had been tapping on the window.

I guess Nana had a plan to keep an eye on Papa after all.

———— ◆ ————

Philip Sullivan is the proud dad of a four-year-old son. He lives in St Petersburg, Florida with his wife Amanda. He is an officer in the Bay Pines Toastmasters Club. He works as an RN at Bay Pines VA hospital.

Spiritual Hide and Seek

Sarah Nolan

I met and married my husband in 2008, about a year and a half after his father Roger had passed away. It's unfortunate that I never got to meet my father-in-law, because it sounds like he was one hell of a guy. He and my husband had an unbreakable bond, one unlike any other I'd ever heard of with a father and a son. Though I never got to meet Roger, I still feel like I've gotten to know him, and luckily, I get the chance to learn more and more with every story that my husband tells me about him.

Evidently Roger was quite a prankster, which is likely where my husband gets it from. From what I've been told, my father-in-law was notorious for taking things, hiding them, and then putting them in the most obvious of places after you'd already looked there. My husband has carried on this tradition, and it drives me mad.

It was with just such an incident that Roger chose to let us know he was still with us. That year, our son desperately wanted a game for the handheld Nintendo DS system for Christmas. My husband and I searched long and hard for the game, and when we finally found it and got it for our son, he was absolutely thrilled. He is our oldest child and only boy, much to his disdain; because of course, his sisters, one of whom is only thirty *seconds* younger than he is, immediately wanted to play his new game on their own DS systems. But he is a sweet kid and he allowed it.

After his twin sister was done playing with the cartridge, she set it down on the couch. At the time, we owned a reclining sofa with all the cushions permanently affixed—nothing detachable, nothing that could get moved or relocated. My daughter said she'd simply placed the game in the middle of one of the couch cushions, and forgot to pick it up when she went to her room. Of course, when we went back to look for it, the thing was gone.

We searched everywhere. EVERYWHERE! We tipped the couch over and dug into all the crevices; we looked in all the air vents, behind the television, under the stove, and behind the toilet. The stupid cartridge was nowhere to be found. My son's heart was broken.

After that, we slowed down our search for the missing game. We didn't give up completely; we just looked less, maybe once a week or so. We couldn't figure out where it had gone. It boggled our minds how we'd torn the house apart to try to find the thing, but it had just disappeared.

One day, about six months after the game was lost, my husband was sitting on the couch while I was in the kitchen, doing who knows what. He got up for a moment, and when he went back to sit down, I heard him say,

"Holy crap!" He came into the kitchen, a look of utter shock and disbelief on his face, and in his hand, was the missing DS game.

We were both blown away. I asked my husband where he'd found it and he said that it had been sitting, just as you please, right in the middle of the sofa cushion.

Everyone in the family had been using this couch for six months. There was nowhere this game could have been hiding, no way it could have suddenly turned up. I looked at the living room picture of my father-in-law, and said, "Good one, Roger!"

That day, Roger let us know that he was still with us, and had been all along. My husband believes that, if his father were still alive, he would be living with us; therefore, we both like to think that he comes along with us whenever we move house. After all, in each of the places we've lived, something has always come up missing, only to be found a few days later in an obvious place. Of course, we always knew that it was just Roger pulling one of his pranks.

Over the past eight years, I've grown to accept and appreciate my father-in-law's ghostly practical jokes. I take them as his way of saying, "I love ya, girl...

———————◆———————

Sarah Nolan is a wife, mom, and would-be writer. She is living in a small town outside of Tampa, working and trying to get her degree. She fancied herself a blogger, but is currently taking time off from that to focus on her rather busy life. Will she make a comeback? Who knows! In the meantime, she spends her time writing for school and just spending time with her husband and three pretty amazing kids in the Florida sunshine!

Wings for Mom
Marie Robinson

Marie Robinson suffered a terrible tragedy when her four-year-old son Jack, died from a brain tumor.

She marked the third anniversary of his passing by visiting his grave in Southern England. While there, she asked her late son to show her a sign and moments later, she noticed a robin flying nearby. Then the robin landed on Jack's headstone and remarkably, hopped onto Marie's hand.

Not only is the word robin in her family's last name, but Jack would look for robins any time he went outside.

She captured the amazing graveside experience on her phone and posted it to Facebook, where millions of people have been moved by it.

Marie, who is overwhelmed by the response to the video, hopes that along with comforting others, it raises awareness about childhood brain tumors, cancer and the grief of losing a child.

Marie Robinson lives in England. Her story has almost 100,000 views on YouTube. She feels blessed that this video has given comfort to so many people.

www.youtube.com/watch?v=mRmj5STsgAU

Mimi's Photo

ERIKA Keen

As long as I can remember, Mimi was one of my favorite people. She coddled me as an infant, watched me learn to roll over and cheered my first steps. I loved her with all my heart. When I was three, I was ecstatic to attend her pre-school. With my lunchbox in hand, I strutted into her classroom for my morning hug. We'd rocked back and forth laughing. Her eyes sparkled when we parted. I loved her contagious laugh.

Mimi was my dad's younger sister. Cancer entered her life at the young age of forty five. She had a mastectomy and we all hoped and prayed she'd be cancer free. She passed away at the age of fifty. Her two teenage daughters were devastated. It was a very sad time for our family.

Years later when I was pregnant, I kept thinking, "I wish Mimi could be here to meet my daughter." I imagined her fussing over Kaylee, just like she did to me. We'd meet at the playground and then have a picnic lunch.

Mimi would cackle with laughter and chase my daughter. Kaylee would hug her tight when she caught her. There would be sleepovers at Aunt Mimi's house that involved chocolate chip pancakes, milkshakes and walks on the beach.

My parents have a photo at their house that has in a place of honor. It's a picture of Mimi after her second daughter was born. There's a bassinette in the background. She's wearing a pink, Minnie Mouse, T-shirt. Her brown hair is cut short and she is glowing. She looks so happy that it hurts my heart to remember that day. Her cheeks are blushed and she in the midst of one of her famous laughs. She looks absolutely the happiest ever.

I felt so sad whenever I looked at that photo. It hurt my heart that my daughters would never feel that special kind of love from Mimi. When my oldest daughter was two, she opened my heart to a new perspective. Every single time we'd visited my parents, she'd dash for that photo. I'd heard that children are more open to the spirit world, because they are still close to it. Now I watched it with my own eyes. She'd hold the frame, smile and talk to Mimi. It was the sweetest thing. She'd offer to share her toys and cookies with her. She took Mimi with her everywhere.

She talked to her, giggled and tucked her in her baby coach to walk with her baby. When it was time for lunch, she brought her to her high chair. She'd glance at Mimi's smiling face while chatting, bouncing her head from side to side, like they were having their very own conversation. They were spiritual buds. Mimi would have loved that.

When my younger daughter, Riley Mae, was born

my thoughts of how much Mimi would have loved both my girls continued. She would have loved Riley's ornery ways. Riley Mae has a dimple in her right cheek. When she smiles, her face lights up and you never know what she's up to. She really does dance like no one is watching. I imagined a dance party with Mimi in her future.

On our last visit to my parent's house, my sister and I honored Mimi. With three bright colored buckets, we headed to the beach to collect the best sea shells with the kids. They searched and scooped and finally filled each pail. My two daughters and my sister's son paraded into the house proud as could be that their mission was completed.

Just like Mimi did for us, we spread out paper on the floor and arranged the paint and brushes. When the shells were cleaned and dry, the three little one dabbed at the blues, reds, purple and oranges to create their masterpieces. I placed the picture of Mimi in the center to watch over the festivities. We'd come full circle. I swore I heard her laughing a few times.

Kaylee was five when she asked to meet Mimi. I had to explain, "Mimi is in Heaven." I had tears in my eyes and Kaylee said "Don't be sad. Look, Mimi is so happy." She held up the photo for proof and smiled. I think Mimi wiped a tear too.

When we leave my mom's house, I put the frame back in place until our next visit. The first thing my girls do when we re-visit is find Mimi and the conversations begin. I can feel her with me watching my girls. I imagine us laughing together at their antics. I know she's near, but I'd really like to hug her just one more time. I might not ever let her go.

Erika Keen is a stay at home mom. She keeps her daughters busy with arts and crafts, dance class, swimming and she volunteers at school. She is known in many circles as the "Baby Whisperer." She's a southern gal who lives in North Carolina with her husband and two big dogs.

Wings and Roots: The Wonder of the Kanoa Tree

Emily Nielsen

My husband, John, would often say hello to our son when he opened the freezer in the garage. Reaching in for a bag of ice or frozen raspberries he'd call out "Hey, Kanoa!" before shutting the door.

It was one of his ways of coping.

I would roll my eyes and maybe giggle - that was mine.

I had giggled, disorienting Demerol coursing through my veins, on the day of my D & C, when John asked the OB if he had a "baggie or something" in which we could carry home the miscarried embryo, which we "knew" was a boy, which we named Kanoa. His question sounded absurd in the setting. But the kind nurse obliged, and Kanoa (Hawaiian for "free man") came home in a specimen cup, in a brown paper bag, and went into the freezer.

A week earlier, the midwife hadn't been able to find the heartbeat of this planned second child. An ultrasound confirmed that the baby had died inside of me at about 10 weeks along. My body just hadn't figured it out yet. It was a difficult time. Kanoa had earned his wings.

But we came through it, and decided that we would commemorate Kanoa by planting him with a tree in the backyard. The ideas started flowing.

"We'll plant it on the little hill above the swing set."

"A big, shady tree."

"With a bench underneath."

"We'll have picnics in the shade. "

That was five years ago. Kanoa's been holed up in the freezer ever since, and his little sister, who decided to ride in on his coat tails (I'm convinced her extra chromosome – Mirabel has Down syndrome - was somehow left for her courtesy of Kanoa), is now four years old.

And then, a few weeks ago, my friend Ron announced on Facebook that he had some catalpa saplings available if any friends were interested. "They're easy to grow!" he claimed. I jumped at the offer -- finally, a tree for Kanoa.

Ron delivered the tree on a Wednesday and I researched how to replant. Trees are very sensitive beings, and I didn't want to mess up the opportunity. Not with all the significance at stake.

My oldest daughter and her cousins helped dig an enormous hole on the little hill above the swing set, and we planted the sapling. It was already a little droopy, but I built the mound for water runoff at the bottom of the hole, surrounded it with rich compost from the garden, and, finally, retrieved Kanoa from his hiding place in the freezer.

John and I gently folded Kanoa into the earth around the tree and each said a little silent blessing. We were finally doing it. We tied a wooden stake to the stalk of the sapling to help it stand tall.

But then, the inevitable happened.

I've often said I have a "black thumb" - no natural gardening ability or special way with plants and flowers here. I've managed to kill just about every piece of green in my care.

And Kanoa's catalpa was no exception.

Within days the bright green leaves had withered and shrunk. The tiny trunk turned brittle. The tree was not thriving. I was devastated.

Mostly, I felt sorry that our dream of commemorating our lost child wouldn't come to fruition. That Kanoa's long and dark stay in our garage freezer was all in vain.

What does it mean? Why is the tree dead? What is my lesson here?

My lesson: Things are not always meant to be, and that's okay. Our best intentions, our most well-thought-out plans, our highest hopes for the right thing to happen... Well, at the very least we held those intentions, we thought out those plans, we hoped for the best. Ride that tide. Believe in your good. It will hang around. There's a lot of it everywhere.

And then.

And then.

Then John was calling from the backyard through the open window to the room where I was folding piles of pink leggings and mismatched socks.

"Come out here! When you can," he said. I took my time. Because laundry.

And when I finally came out, I saw.

The leaves were tiny, and the bright green of spring. They were spurting from the base of the lifeless catalpa like heart-shaped butterflies having a huddle. Dozens of them.

Life. Growing.

Neither John nor I knew why we had left the reedy dry brown tree in the hole. We just did. Perhaps our hearts just knew. Perhaps we were waiting to see what else might grow. Perhaps we couldn't bear the thought of turning up that soil.

Last week, we had to have an old and heavy apple tree removed from the yard. While he was there, John asked the arborist to come take a look at our surprisingly sprouting catalpa. What had made it start to grow again?

The arborist looked squarely at my husband and said, "I think you know."

My lesson: Continue to believe that good things are happening. Everywhere, all the time. That what we hope and think and intend can indeed unfurl into the light of a bright day.

Catalpa trees grow large and green. They have white blossoms in the spring, and long funny bean pods in the summer. Soon, we will have a picnic under the Kanoa Tree in our backyard, our very own tree that signifies strength and freedom. Feel free to come on over and say hey.

———— ◆ ————

Emily Nielsen is the owner of Balance Family Fitness in Boise, Idaho, and is committed to a holistic approach to wellness and healthy nutrition. She is an AFAA Certified Personal Trainer, an ACE Certified Group Fitness Instructor, and a retreat facilitator. Her popular classes include online motivational programs and "Ommm on the Range" Goat Yoga at her urban farm retreat. Find more details at www.balancefamilyfitness.com.

BOOKS BY MILL PARK PUBLISHING

eBook and Audiobook
Midlife Happy Hour

Paperback, eBook, and Audiobook
Gators & Taters

Paperback and eBook
Angel Bumps
Midlife Cabernet
Feisty after 45
The Magic Potato – La Papa Mágica
Drinking with Dead Women Writers
Drinking with Dead Drunks
The Angel of Esperança
Mother Knows Better
Little White Dress

Paperback
The Red Tease
Daily Erotica
Mother Knows Best
The Backyard Chicken Fight